A Narrative of the Life of Mrs. Mary Jemison

LAURENCE M. HAUPTMAN, SERIES EDITOR

This memorial statue to Mary Jemison stands in Letchworth State Park in the Genesee River Valley, New York. It is reproduced with the kind permission of the Rochester Museum of Arts and Sciences.

A NARRATIVE

OF THE LIFE OF

MRS. MARY JEMISON,

Who was taken by the Indians, in the year 1755,
when only about twelve years of age, and
has continued to reside amongst
them to the present time.

CONTAINING

An ACCOUNT of the Murder of her Father and his
Family; her sufferings; her marriage to two Indians;
her troubles with her Children; barbarities of the Indians in the French and Revolutionary Wars; the life
of her last Husband, &c.; and many Historical Facts
never before published.
Carefully taken from her own words, Nov. 29th, 1823.

TO WHICH IS ADDED,

An APPENDIX, containing an account of the tragedy at
the Devil's Hole, in 1763, and of Sullivan's Expedition; the Traditions, Manners, Customs, &c. of the Indians, as believed and practised at the present day,
and since Mrs. Jemison's captivity; together with
some Anecdotes, and other entertaining matter.

❖◉❖◉❖

BY JAMES E. SEAVER.

❖◉❖◉❖

Foreword by George Abrams

SYRACUSE UNIVERSITY PRESS

Foreword to the 1990 edition copyright © by Syracuse University Press
Syracuse, New York 13244-5160

All Rights Reserved

First Edition 1990

05 04 03 02 01   7 8 9 10 11

With the exception of the foreword, this book is reprinted from the
Peter Smith edition, published in 1975.

The paper used in this publication meets the minimum
requirements of American National Standard for Information
Sciences–Permanence of Paper for Printed Library Materials,
ANSI Z39.48-1984. ∞™

Library of Congress Cataloging-in-Publication Data

Seaver, James E. (James Everett), 1787–1827.
    A narrative of the life of Mrs. Mary Jemison / James E. Seaver ;
foreword by George Abrams.
       p.   cm. — The Iroquois and their neighbors
    "With the exception of the foreword, this book is reprinted from
the Peter Smith edition, published in 1975"—T.p. verso.
    ISBN 0-8156-2491-3 (alk. paper)
    1. Jemison, Mary 1743–1833. 2. Seneca Indians—Captivities.
3. Pioneers—Genesee River Valley (Pa. and N.Y.)—Biography.
4. Genesee River Valley (Pa. and N.Y.)—Biography. I. Title.
II. Series.
E83.J46S42   1990
974.7'8800497502—dc20
[B]   90-31334
                                                             CIP

Manufactured in the United States of America

CONTENTS.

❖⊂⊃❖⊂⊃❖

FOREWORD.

❖⊙❖⊙❖

AMONG the most famous of Indian captives is Mary Jemison, a Scots-Irish immigrant girl who was captured on the advancing western frontier of central Pennsylvania. Her story, first published in 1824 at Canandaigua, New York, was recorded by Dr. James Everett Seaver following an interview by Seaver of Mary Jemison on November 29th, 1823, several years before her death. This remarkable narrative of the long and eventful life of Mary Jemison spans the important period of Seneca history from the French and Indian War, through the American Revolution, the beginning of the treaty period, to the establishment of Seneca reservations in western New York.

It was the religious intolerance, political turmoil, and economic hardship in Europe in the mid-1700s that resulted in the emigration of Mary Jemison's family from Londonderry, Ireland. Sailing aboard the ship *William and Mary*, probably in the year 1742, Mary was born on the Atlantic Ocean during the voyage. The family landed at Philadelphia and eventually settled on Marsh Creek near what is now Carlisle, Pennsylvania, where additional children were born to Thomas and Jane Erwin Jemison.

Following the murder of Mary's family and her capture in 1758 by a group of Shawnee Indians and Frenchmen, she was taken to the Ohio River. There she was adopted and given an Indian name by two Seneca women who had suffered the loss of a brother in the war. It was often the custom at the time for families to "replace" a person lost in battle by adopting a captive taken in warfare. Mary's adoption signified her acceptance into the ranks of the Seneca, and her Seneca name, which has been variously transcribed but is translated as "Two Falling Voices," indicated the end of sorrow for the two women who adopted her. From genealogical data, it appears most likely that she was adopted into the heron clan. Her Seneca name also appears to have been one which was created for the unique circumstance which surround her becoming a member of the tribe. Normally, as is presently the case, tribal members would be given one of a body of names belonging to each clan. In contemporary times, her name has been given to two females, both descendants of the captive, one in the heron clan and one an adopted member of the wolf clan. Her surname of Jemison also marks the early appearance of such English names among the Seneca.

Mary Jemison, although born into the

white world where she lived some sixteen years, became a Seneca in terms of her culture and, in addition, her immediate descendants were legally recognized Seneca people. This is important especially in the case of her son Thomas because he had no Seneca ancestry, being a mixture of white and Delaware. Although the various Iroquois tribes in New York adhere to a strict matrilineal descent in determining tribal membership today, such was not the case in the late 1700s and early 1800s, when numerous individuals were adopted into the ranks of the various Iroquois tribes long before the first recording of tribal enrollments. Mary, her children, and the children of her daughters were culturally and legally recognized as Senecas, as are her matrilineal descendants today.

At present, there are literally thousands of descendants of Mary Jemison, primarily among the Seneca but also represented in all of the other tribes of the Iroquois. Her surname survives among her descendants in a half-dozen forms, from the original Jemison, to Jimerson, Jimmerson, Jamieson, and others. These variant forms date from the time when many descendants were illiterate and accepted whatever spelling government agents and census takers gave to their name. Jemison descendants are generally very proud of their ancestor, and many attend annual late-summer festivities held at Letchworth Park, the site of the former Gardeau

Reservation. Others deny descent from Mary
Jemison, choosing to reject any claim of non-
Indian, or non-Seneca, ancestry.

The creation of the Gardeau Reservation
as a personal grant to Mary Jemison follows
the pattern that had been established by the
grants that had been personally given to
Cornplanter by the Commonwealth of Pennsylvania, and the attempt by Handsome
Lake to secure a similar grant for the Oil
Spring Reservation. In Mary Jemison's case,
however, the granting to her of the reservation, which was carved out of Seneca lands,
showed the respect and gratitude felt toward
Mary by the other Seneca. Her efforts as in-
termediary between the Seneca and the
whites and her refusal to return to her white
family when given the opportunity war-
ranted her this honor.

Mary, a contemporary of such famous Iroquois personalities as Cornplanter, Red
Jacket, Governor Blacksnake, Handsome
Lake, Joseph Brant, and other well-known
white captives, such as Horatio Jones and
Peter Crouse, emerges as one of the few females to gain prominence and recognition in
the history of the Seneca, owing in large part
to the interest of Dr. James Seaver and William Pryor Letchworth. Indeed, Mary is
among the most famous of all female captives, and certainly is the best known of any
of the Seneca captives, who numbered in the
hundreds. Her story has captured the atten-

tion of Indian and non-Indian alike, giving rise to outdoor dramas and novels about her life. Monuments have been erected to her memory, both at Letchworth Park and in Pennsylvania. The Daughters of the American Revolution have named a chapter for her, even though the Seneca supported the British in the war.

Jemison's greatest joy, as well as her greatest sorrow, derived from her eight children. She married a Delaware Indian while still living along the Ohio, and their first child, a girl, died when only a few days old, an event Mary related with great sadness to her biographer. Her second child, also half Delaware, she named Thomas Jemison after her father. Because the Delaware were closely associated with the Seneca along the Ohio and Allegany rivers during the mid 1700s, there was a great deal of intermarriage between tribes, especially on the Cattaraugus Reservation where the present-day Delaware, known as the Munsees, still reside.

Following the birth of Thomas and her husband's departure to the Cherokee wars, Mary made a journey of hundreds of miles to join her adopted Seneca family on the Genesee River, the homeland of the Seneca. It was this arduous journey that carried her up the Ohio and Allegany rivers into the Genesee River system, which is depicted in the famous statue of Mary carrying her son

in a cradleboard, presently located in Letchworth Park.

It is interesting to note that in regard to
the Seneca conception of geography there
was no differentiation in terms of place-
names between the Ohio and Allegany
rivers. The latter name was derived from an
Algonquian language, the former is a Seneca
term, O-He-Yoh (Beautiful River), which ap-
plies to the entire drainage from the headwaters of the Allegany to the Mississippi. In
traversing the Ohio to the headwaters of the
Genesee, Mary Jemison passed through various Seneca villages. Some place-names mentioned by Jemison have still not been as-
signed to specific localities.

The death of her Delaware husband in the
Cherokee wars necessitated that she, as a
young woman with a small child, be remar-
ried. Her marriage with Hiokatoo, an older,
well-established and respected Seneca
leader, was arranged. Mary and Hiokatoo
had six children, one of whom, Jane, died as
a young woman. All of her other children
who survived into adulthood left numerous
descendants.

Mary Jemison related to Seaver many
events that occurred during her life among
the Seneca, beginning with the so-called
massacre at Devil's Hole in 1793, shortly after her arrival on the Genesee. She told of
her traumatic experiences during the American Revolution when the power and organi-

zation of the Iroquois Confederacy was challenged, including the invasion of Seneca territory by General John Sullivan in 1779 that drove the majority of Seneca to seek refuge with the British at Fort Niagara, one of the darkest periods in Seneca history.

With the conclusion of peace and the beginning of a series of land cessions by the Seneca, the reservation period began. Mary was granted a separate piece of land in these treaty negotiations, the Gardeau Reservation where she had resided since her arrival on the Genesee River. There she remained with her family and friends until increasing white pressure was placed upon the Seneca to sell the numerous Genesee River reservations and remove west. It was during this period that Mary Jemison achieved the distinction in Seneca history of becoming the only woman signatory to an Iroquois treaty. Eventually, in 1831 Mary left the Gardeau Reservation to live among the other Seneca and members of her family who had relocated to the Buffalo Creek Reservation where, on September 19, 1833, she died. She was buried in the Mission Cemetery, the resting place of many well-known residents of the reservation.

The Buffalo industrialist William Pryor Letchworth took great interest in the story of Mary Jemison. Eventually, he was to create Letchworth Park from the property that he had acquired around his home at Glen Iris at

the brink of the gorge. Letchworth had the
old Caneadea council house removed from
the former Caneadea Reservation to Glen
Iris and rededicated in 1872. At that time
Letchworth was also adopted into the Seneca
Nation, a member of the wolf clan with the
name that translates as "the man who does
the right thing."

Letchworth had the remains of Mary
Jemison removed to Glen Iris in 1874 and re-
interred with a great ceremony attended by a
delegation of her descendants. The relocation
of her grave was also necessitated by the ille-
gal sale of the Buffalo Creek Reservation in
1838 and by the gradual encroachment of the
City of Buffalo on the former reservation.
This resulted in the Mission Cemetery,
which had been on the reservation, being
eventually relocated at Forest Lawn Cemetery in Buffalo. This was the occasion also for
the relocation of the graves of renowned
Seneca, such as Red Jacket. Letchworth, con-
cerned about the fate of Mary Jemison's remains, wished to have them returned to the
site of her former home on the banks of the
Genesee. Finally, a heroic statue of Mary
and her infant son, Thomas was commissioned by Letchworth and erected in 1910 at
the site of her reburial on the anniversary of
her death. Unfortunately, Letchworth was
too ill to be present, dying in December of
that year.

Jemison's importance in the history of the

Seneca derives from her having been an ob-
server of a critical period for the Iroquois.
Fortunately for the historic record, her obser-
vations as recorded by James Seaver offer a
unique opportunity to learn about what
Seneca life was like at that time. Seaver, a
rather mysterious figure in his own right,
must have been motivated to seek out Mary
Jemison because of his proximity to her and
his interest in local Indian history, especially
that of this extraordinary woman. Although
Seaver has Jemison speaking in the first person in this account, the narrative reflects the
ideas and words of both Seaver and the subject of his story. Seaver's efforts have left us
not only with a unique and valuable record
of an important period of Iroquois history but
also his work stands among the best accounts
and is a major contribution to the literature
of Indian captivities.

GEORGE H. J. ABRAMS
Special Assistant to the Director
Museum of the American Indian

PREFACE.

❖◐❖◯❖

THAT to biographical writings we are indebted
for the greatest and best field in which to study
mankind, or human nature, is a fact duly appreci-
ated by a well-informed community. In them we
can trace the effects of mental operations to their
proper sources; and by comparing our own composition with that of those who have excelled in
virtue, or with that of those who have been sunk
in the lowest depths of folly and vice, we are enabled to select a plan of life that will at least
afford self-satisfaction, and guide us through the
world in paths of morality.

Without a knowledge of the lives of the vile and
abandoned, we should be wholly incompetent to
set an appropriate value upon the charms, the
excellence and the worth of those principles which
have produced the finest traits in the character of
the most virtuous.

Biography is a telescope of life, through which
we can see the extremes and excesses of the varied
properties of the human heart. Wisdom and folly,
refinement and vulgarity, love and hatred, tenderness and cruelty, happiness and misery, piety and
infidelity, commingled with every other cardinal
virtue or vice, are to be seen on the variegated

xvii

pages of the history of human events, and are eminently deserving the attention of those who would learn to walk in the "paths of peace."

The brazen statue and the sculptured marble, can commemorate the greatness of heroes, statesmen, philosophers, and blood-stained conquerors, who have risen to the zenith of human glory and popularity, under the influence of the mild sun of prosperity: but it is the faithful page of biography that transmits to future generations the poverty, pain, wrong, hunger, wretchedness and torment, and every nameless misery that has been endured by those who have lived in obscurity, and groped their lonely way through a long series of unpropitious events, with but little help besides the light of nature. While the gilded monument displays in brightest colors the vanity of pomp, and the emptiness of nominal greatness, the biographical page, that lives in every line, is giving lessons of fortitude in time of danger, patience in suffering, hope in distress, invention in necessity, and resignation to unavoidable evils. Here also may be learned, pity for the bereaved, benevolence for the destitute, and compassion for the helpless; and at the same time all the sympathies of the soul will be naturally excited to sigh at the unfavorable result, or to smile at the fortunate relief.

In the great inexplicable chain which forms the circle of human events, each individual link is placed on a level with the others, and performs an equal task; but, as the world is partial, it is the situation that attracts the attention of mankind, and excites the unfortunate vociferous eclat of elevation, that raises the pampered parasite to such an immense height in the scale of personal vanity, as, generally, to deprive him of respect, before he can return to a state of equilibrium with his fellows, or to the place whence he started.

Few great men have passed from the stage of action, who have not left in the history of their lives indelible marks of ambition or folly, which produced insurmountable reverses, and rendered the whole a mere caricature, that can be examined only with disgust and regret. Such pictures, however, are profitable, for "by others' faults wise men correct their own."

The following is a piece of biography, that shows what changes may be effected in the animal and mental constitution of man; what trials may be surmounted; what cruelties perpetrated, and what pain endured, when stern necessity holds the reins, and drives the car of fate.

As books of this kind are sought and read with avidity, especially by children, and are well calculated to excite their attention, inform their understanding, and improve them in the art of reading, the greatest care has been observed to render the style easy, the language comprehensive, and the description natural. Prolixity has been studiously avoided. The line of distinction between virtue and vice has been rendered distinctly visible; and chastity of expression and sentiment have received due attention. Strict fidelity has been observed in the composition: consequently, no circumstance has been intentionally exaggerated by the paintings of fancy, nor by fine flashes of rhetoric: neither has the picture been rendered more dull than the original. Without the aid of fiction, what was received as matter of fact, only has been recorded.

It will be observed that the subject of this narrative has arrived at least to the advanced age of eighty years; that she is destitute of education; and that her journey of life, throughout its texture, has been interwoven with troubles, which ordinarily are calculated to impair the faculties of the mind; and it will be remembered, that there are but few old people who can recollect with precision the circumstances of their lives, (particularly those circumstances which transpired after middle age.) If, therefore, any error shall be discovered in the narration in respect to time, it will be overlooked by the kind reader, or charitably placed to the narrator's account, and not imputed to neglect, or to the want of attention in the compiler.

The appendix is principally taken from the words of Mrs. Jemison's statements. Those parts which were not derived from her, are deserving equal credit, having been obtained from authentic sources.

For the accommodation of the reader, the work has been divided into chapters, with a list of contents prefixed. The introduction will facilitate the understanding of what follows; and as it contains matter that could not be inserted with propriety in any other place, will be read with interest and satisfaction.

Having finished my undertaking, the subsequent pages are cheerfully submitted to the perusal and

approbation or animadversion of a candid, generous and indulgent public. At the same time it is
fondly hoped that the lessons of distress that are
pourtrayed, may have a direct tendency to increase our love of liberty; to enlarge our views of
the blessings that are derived from our liberal in-
stitutions; and to excite in our breasts sentiments
of devotion and gratitude to the great Author and
finisher of our happiness.

THE AUTHOR.

Pembroke, March 1, 1824.

INTRODUCTION.

❖◎❖◎❖

THE Peace of 1783, and the consequent cessation of Indian hostilities and barbarities, returned to their friends those prisoners, who had escaped the tomahawk, the gauntlet, and the savage fire, after their having spent many years in captivity, and restored harmony to society.

The stories of Indian cruelties which were common in the new settlements, and were calamitous realities previous to that propitious event; slumbered in the minds that had been constantly agitated by them, and were only roused occasionally, to become the fearful topic of the fireside.

It is presumed that at this time there are but few native Americans that have arrived to middle age, who cannot distinctly recollect of sitting in the chimney corner when children, all contracted with fear, and there listening to their parents or visitors, while they related stories of Indian conquests, and murders, that would make their flaxen hair nearly stand erect, and almost destroy the power of motion.

At the close of the Revolutionary war; all that

part of the State of New-York that lies west of
Utica was uninhabited by white people, and few
indeed had ever passed beyond Fort Stanwix, except when engaged in war against the Indians, who
were numerous, and occupied a number of large
towns between the Mohawk river and lake Erie.
Sometime elapsed after this event, before the country about the lakes and on the Genesee river was
visited, save by an occasional land speculator, or
by defaulters who wished by retreating to what in
those days was deemed almost the end of the earth,
to escape the force of civil law.

At length, the richness and fertility of the soil
excited emigration, and here and there a family
settled down and commenced improvements in the
country which had recently been the property of
the aborigines. Those who settled near the Genesee
river, soon became acquainted with "The White
Woman," as Mrs. Jemison is called, whose history
they anxiously sought, both as a matter of interest and curiosity. Frankness characterized her
conduct, and without reserve she would readily
gratify them by relating some of the most important periods of her life.

Although her bosom companion was an ancient
Indian warrior, and notwithstanding her children
and associates were all Indians, yet it was found
that she possessed an uncommon share of hospi-
tality, and that her friendship was well worth
courting and preserving. Her house was the stranger's home; from her table the hungry were re-
freshed;—she made the naked as comfortable as
her means would admit of; and in all her actions,

discovered so much natural goodness of heart, that her admirers increased in proportion to the extension of her acquaintance, and she became celebrated as the friend of the distressed. She was the protectress of the homeless fugitive, and made welcome the weary wanderer. Many still live to commemorate her benevolence towards them, when prisoners during the war, and to ascribe their deliverance to the mediation of "The White Woman."

The settlements increased, and the whole country around her was inhabited by a rich and respectable people, principally from New-England, as much distinguished for their spirit of inquisitiveness as for their habits of industry and honesty, who had all heard from one source and another a part of her life in detached pieces, and had obtained an idea that the whole taken in connection would afford instruction and amusement.

Many gentlemen of respectability, felt anxious that her narrative might be laid before the public, with a view not only to perpetuate the remembrance of the atrocities of the savages in former times, but to preserve some historical facts which they supposed to be intimately connected with her life, and which otherwise must be lost.

Forty years had passed since the close of the Revolutionary war, and almost seventy years had seen Mrs. Jemison with the Indians, when Daniel W. Banister, Esq. at the instance of several gentlemen, and prompted by his own ambition to add something to the accumulating fund of useful knowledge, resolved, in the autumn of 1823, to embrace that time, while she was capable of recol-

lecting and reciting the scenes through which
she had passed, to collect from herself, and to publish to the world, an accurate account of her life.
I was employed to collect the materials, and
prepare the work for the press; and accordingly
went to the house of Mrs. Jennet Whaley in the
town of Castile, Genesee co. N. Y. in company
with the publisher, who procured the interesting
subject of the following narrative, to come to that
place (a distance of four miles) and there repeat
the story of her evèntful life. She came on foot in
company with Mr. Thomas Clute, whom she considers her protector, and tarried almost three days,
which time was busily occupied in taking a sketch
of her narrative as she recited it.

Her appearance was well calculated to excite a
great degree of sympathy in a stranger, who had
been partially informed of her origin, when comparing her present situation with what it probably
would have been, had she been permitted to have
remained with her friends, and to have enjoyed
the blessings of civilization.

In stature she is very short, and considerably
under the middle size, and stands tolerably erect,
with her head bent forward, apparently from her
having for a long time been accustomed to carrying heavy burdens in a strap placed across her forehead. Her complexion is very white for a woman
of her age, and although the wrinkles of fourscore
years are deeply indented in her cheeks, yet the
crimson of youth is distinctly visible. Her eyes are
light blue, a little faded by age, and naturally
brilliant and sparkling. Her sight is quite dim,

though she is able to perform her necessary labor without the assistance of glasses. Her cheek bones are high, and rather prominent, and her front teeth, in the lower jaw, are sound and good. When she looks up and is engaged in conversation her countenance is very expressive; but from her long residence with the Indians, she has acquired the habit of peeping from under eye-brows as they do with the head inclined downwards. Formerly her hair was of a light chesnut brown—it is now quite grey, a little curled, of middling length and tied in a bunch behind. She informed me that she had never worn a cap nor a comb.

She speaks English plainly and distinctly, with a little of the Irish emphasis, and has the use of words so well as to render herself intelligible on any subject with which she is acquainted. Her recollection and memory exceeded my expectation. It cannot be reasonably supposed, that a person of her age has kept the events of seventy years in so complete a chain as to be able to assign to each its proper time and place; she, however, made her recital with as few obvious mistakes as might be found in that of a person of fifty.

She walks with a quick step without a staff, and I was informed by Mr. Clute, that she could yet cross a stream on a log or pole as steadily as any other person.

Her passions are easily excited. At a number of periods in her narration, tears trickled down her grief worn cheek, and at the same time a rising sigh would stop her utterance.

Industry is a virtue which she has uniformly

practised from the day of her adoption to the present. She pounds her samp, cooks for herself, gathers and chops wood, feeds her cattle and poultry, and performs other laborious services. Last season she planted, tended and gathered corn—in short, she is always busy.

Her dress at the time I saw her, was made and worn after the Indian fashion, and consisted of a shirt, short gown, petticoat, stockings, moccasins, a blanket and a bonnet. The shirt was of cotton and made at the top, as I was informed, like a man's without collar or sleeves—was open before and extended down about midway of the hips.— The petticoat was a piece of broadcloth with the list at the top and bottom and the ends sewed together. This was tied on by a string that was passed over it and around the waist, in such a manner as to let the bottom of the petticoat down half way between the knee and ankle and leave one-fourth of a yard at the top to be turned down over the string—the bottom of the shirt coming a little below, and on the outside of the top of the fold so as to leave the list and two or three inches of the cloth uncovered. The stockings, were of blue broadcloth, tied, or pinned on, which reached from the knees, into the mouth of the moccasins.— Around her toes only she had some rags, and over these her buckskin moccasins. Her gown was of undressed flannel, colored brown. It was made in old yankee style, with long sleeves, covered the top of the hips, and was tied before in two places with strings of deer skin. Over all this, she wore an Indian blanket. On her head she wore a piece of old brown woollen cloth made somewhat like a sun bonnet.

Such was the dress that this woman was contented to wear, and habit had rendered it convenient and comfortable. She wore it not as a matter of necessity, but from choice, for it will be seen in the sequel, that her property is sufficient to enable her to dress in the best fashion, and to allow her every comfort of life.

Her house, in which she lives, is 20 by 28 feet; built of square timber, with a shingled roof, and a framed stoop. In the centre of the house is a chimney of stones and sticks, in which there are two fire places. She has a good framed barn, 26 by 36, well filled, and owns a fine stock of cattle and horses. Besides the buildings above mentioned, she owns a number of houses that are occupied by tenants, who work her flats upon shares.

Her dwelling, is about one hundred rods north of the Great Slide, a curiosity that will be described in its proper place, on the west side of the Genesee river.

Mrs. Jemison, appeared sensible of her ignorance of the manners of the white people, and for that reason, was not familiar, except with those with whom she was intimately acquainted. In fact she was (to appearance) so jealous of her rights, or that she should say something that would be injurious to herself or family, that if Mr. Clute had not been present, we should have been unable to have obtained her history. She, however, soon became free and unembarrassed in her conversation, and spoke with a degree of mildness, candor and simplicity, that is calculated to remove all doubts as to the veracity of the speaker. The vices of the Indians, she appeared disposed not to aggravate, and seemed to take pride in extoling their virtues. A kind of family pride inclined her to withhold whatever would blot the character of her descendants, and perhaps induced her to keep back many things that would have been interesting.

For the life of her last husband, we are indebted to her cousin, Mr. George Jemison, to whom she referred us for information on that subject generally. The thoughts of his deeds, probably chilled her old heart, and made her dread to rehearse them, and at the same time she well knew they were no secret, for she had frequently heard him relate the whole, not only to her cousin, but to others.

Before she left us she was very sociable, and she resumed her naturally pleasant countenance, enlivened with a smile.

Her neighbors speak of her as possessing one of the happiest tempers and dispositions, and give her the name of never having done a censurable act to their knowledge.

Her habits, are those of the Indians—she sleeps on skins without a bedstead, sits upon the floor or on a bench, and holds her victuals on her lap, or in her hands.

Her ideas of religion, correspond in every respect with those of the great mass of the Senecas. She applauds virtue, and despises vice. She believes in a future state, in which the good will be happy, and the bad miserable; and that the acquisition of that happiness, depends primarily upon human volition, and the consequent good deeds of the happy recipient of blessedness. The doctrines taught in the Christian religion, she is a stranger to.

Her daughters are said to be active and enterprizing women, and her grandsons, who arrived to manhood, are considered able, decent and respectable men in their tribe.

Having in this cursory manner, introduced the subject of the following pages, I proceed to the narration of a life that has been viewed with attention, for a great number of years by a few, and which will be read by the public with the mixed sensations of pleasure and pain, and with interest, anxiety and satisfaction.

LIFE

OF

MARY JEMISON.

✧◎✧◎✧

CHAPTER I.

Nativity of her Parents. Their removal to America.
Her Birth. Parents settle in Pennsylvania.
Omen of her Captivity.

ALTHOUGH I may have frequently heard the
history of my ancestry, my recollection is too im-
perfect to enable me to trace it further back than
to my father and mother, whom I have often heard
mention the families from whence they originated,
as having possessed wealth and honorable stations
under the government of the country in which
they resided.

On the account of the great length of time that
has elapsed since I was separated from my parents
and friends, and having heard the story of their nativity only in the days of my childhood, I am not
able to state positively, which of the two countries,
Ireland or Scotland, was the land of my parents'
birth and education. It, however, is my impression,
that they were born and brought up in Ireland.

My Father's name was Thomas Jemison, and

my mother's, before her marriage with him, was
Jane Erwin. Their affection for each other was mutual, and of that happy kind which tends directly
to sweeten the cup of life; to render connubial
sorrows lighter; to assuage every discontentment;
and to promote not only their own comfort, but
that of all who come within the circle of their acquaintance. Of their happiness I recollect to have
heard them speak; and the remembrance I yet retain of their mildness and perfect agreement in the
government of their children, together with their
mutual attention to our common education, manners, religious instruction and wants, renders it a
fact in my mind, that they were ornaments to the
married state, and examples of connubial love,
worthy of imitation. After my remembrance, they
were strict observers of religious duties; for it was
the daily practice of my father, morning and evening, to attend, in his family, to the worship of God.

Resolved to leave the land of their nativity,
they removed from their residence to a port in Ireland, where they lived but a short time before they
set sail for this country, in the year 1742 or 3, on
board the ship Mary William, bound to Philadelphia, in the state of Pennsylvania.

The intestine divisions, civil wars, and ecclesiastical rigidity and domination that prevailed in
those days, were the causes of their leaving their
mother country, to find a home in the American
wilderness, under the mild and temperate government of the descendants of William Penn; where,
without fear, they might worship God, and perform their usual avocations.

In Europe my parents had two sons and one daughter, whose names were John, Thomas and Betsey; with whom, after having put their effects on board, they embarked, leaving a large connexion of relatives and friends, under all those painful sensations, which are only felt when kindred souls give the parting hand and last farewell to those to whom they are endeared by every friendly tie.

In the course of their voyage I was born, to be the sport of fortune and almost an outcast to civil society; to stem the current of adversity through a long chain of vicissitudes, unsupported by the advice of tender parents, or the hand of an affectionate friend; and even without the enjoyment, from others, of any of those tender sympathies that are adapted to the sweetening of society, except such as naturally flow from uncultivated minds, that have been calloused by ferocity.

Excepting my birth, nothing remarkable occurred to my parents on their passage, and they were safely landed at Philadelphia. My father being fond of rural life, and having been bred to agricultural pursuits, soon left the city, and removed his family to the then frontier settlements of Pennsylvania, to a tract of excellent land lying on Marsh creek. At that place he cleared a large farm, and for seven or eight years enjoyed the fruits of his industry. Peace attended their labors; and they had nothing to alarm them, save the midnight howl of the prowling wolf, or the terrifying shriek of the ferocious panther, as they occasionally visited their improvements, to take a lamb or a calf to satisfy their hunger.

During this period my mother had two sons, between whose ages there was a difference of about three years: the oldest was named Matthew, and the other Robert.

Health presided on every countenance, and vigor and strength characterized every exertion. Our mansion was a little paradise. The morning of my childish, happy days, will ever stand fresh in my remembrance, notwithstanding the many severe trials through which I have passed, in arriving at my present situation, at so advanced an age. Even at this remote period, the recollection of my pleasant home at my father's, of my parents, of my brothers and sister, and of the manner in which I was deprived of them all at once, affects me so powerfully, that I am almost overwhelmed with grief, that is seemingly insupportable. Frequently I dream of those happy days: but, alas! they are gone: they have left me to be carried through a long life, dependent for the little pleasures of nearly seventy years, upon the tender mercies of the Indians! In the spring of 1752, and through the succeeding seasons, the stories of Indian barbarities inflicted upon the whites in those days, frequently excited in my parents the most serious alarm for our safety.

The next year the storm gathered faster; many murders were committed; and many captives were exposed to meet death in its most frightful form, by having their bodies stuck full of pine splinters, which were immediately set on fire, while their tormentors, exulting in their distress, would rejoice at their agony!

In 1754, an army for the protection of the settlers, and to drive back the French and Indians, was raised from the militia of the colonial governments, and placed (secondarily) under the command of Col. George Washington. In that army I had an uncle, whose name was John Jemison, who was killed at the battle at the Great Meadows, or Fort Necessity. His wife had died some time before this, and left a young child, which my mother nursed in the most tender manner, till its mother's sister took it away, a few months after my uncle's death. The French and Indians, after the surrender of Fort Necessity by Col. Washington, (which happened the same season, and soon after his victory over them at that place,) grew more and more terrible. The death of the whites, and plundering and burning their property, was apparently their only object: But as yet we had not heard the death-yell, nor seen the smoke of a dwelling that had been lit by an Indian's hand.

The return of a new-year's day found us unmolested; and though we knew that the enemy was at no great distance from us, my father concluded that he would continue to occupy his land another season: expecting (probably from the great exertions which the government was then making) that as soon as the troops could commence their operations in the spring, the enemy would be conquered and compelled to agree to a treaty of peace.

In the preceding autumn my father either moved to another part of his farm, or to another neighborhood, a short distance from our former abode. I well recollect moving, and that the barn that was on the place we moved to was built of logs, though the house was a good one.

The winter of 1754–5 was as mild as a common fall season, and the spring presented a pleasant seed time, and indicated a plenteous harvest. My father, with the assistance of his oldest sons, repaired his farm as usual, and was daily preparing the soil for the reception of the seed. His cattle and sheep were numerous, and according to the best idea of wealth that I can now form, he was wealthy.

But alas! how transitory are all human affairs! how fleeting are riches! how brittle the invisible thread on which all earthly comforts are suspended! Peace in a moment can take an immeasurable flight; health can lose its rosy cheeks; and life will vanish like a vapor at the appearance of the sun! In one fatal day our prospects were all blasted; and death, by cruel hands, inflicted upon almost the whole of the family.

On a pleasant day in the spring of 1755, when my father was sowing flax-seed, and my brothers driving the teams, I was sent to a neighbor's house, a distance of perhaps a mile, to procure a horse and return with it the next morning. I went as I was directed. I was out of the house in the beginning of the evening, and saw a sheet wide spread approaching towards me, in which I was caught (as I have ever since believed) and deprived of my senses! The family soon found me on the ground, almost lifeless, (as they said,) took me in, and made use of every remedy in their power for my recovery, but without effect till day-break, when my senses returned, and I soon found myself in good health, so that I went home with the horse very early in the morning.

The appearance of that sheet, I have ever considered as a forerunner of the melancholy catastrophe that so soon afterwards happened to our family: and my being caught in it, I believe, was ominous of my preservation from death at the time we were captured.

❖○❖○❖

CHAPTER II.

Her Education. Captivity. Journey to Fort Pitt. Mother's Farewell Address. Murder of her Family. Preparation of the Scalps. Indian Precautions. Arrival at Fort Pitt, &c.

MY education had received as much attention from my parents, as their situation in a new country would admit of. I had been at school some, where I learned to read in a book that was about half as large as a Bible; and in the Bible I had read a little. I had also learned the Catechism, which I used frequently to repeat to my parents, and every night, before I went to bed, I was obliged to stand up before my mother and repeat some words that I suppose was a prayer.

My reading, Catechism and prayers, I have long since forgotten; though for a number of the first years that I lived with the Indians, I repeated the prayers as often as I had an opportunity. After the revolutionary war, I remembered the names of some of the letters when I saw them; but have never read a word since I was taken prisoner. It is but a few years since a Missionary kindly gave me a Bible, which I am very fond of hearing my neighbors read to me, and should be pleased to learn to read it myself; but my sight has been for a number of years, so dim that I have not been able to distinguish one letter from another.

As I before observed, I got home with the horse very early in the morning, where I found a man that lived in our neighborhood, and his sister-in-law who had three children, one son and two daughters. I soon learned that they had come there to live a short time; but for what purpose I cannot say. The woman's husband, however, was at that time in Washington's army, fighting for his country; and as her brother-in-law had a house she had lived with him in his absence. Their names I have forgotten.

Immediately after I got home, the man took the horse to go to his house after a bag of grain, and took his gun in his hand for the purpose of killing game, if he should chance to see any.—Our family, as usual, was busily employed about their common business. Father was shaving an axe-helve at the side of the house; mother was making preparations for breakfast;—my two oldest brothers were at work near the barn; and the little ones, with myself, and the woman and her three children, were in the house.

Breakfast was not yet ready, when we were alarmed by the discharge of a number of guns, that seemed to be near. Mother and the women before mentioned, almost fainted at the report, and every one trembled with fear. On opening the door, the man and horse lay dead near the house, having just been shot by the Indians.

[8]

I was afterwards informed, that the Indians discovered him at his own house with his gun, and pursued him to father's, where they shot him as I have related. They first secured my father, and then rushed into the house, and without the least resistance made prisoners of my mother, Robert, Matthew, Betsey, the woman and her three children, and myself, and then commenced plundering.

My two brothers, Thomas and John, being at the barn, escaped and went to Virginia, where my grandfather Erwin then lived, as I was informed by a Mr. Fields, who was at my house about the close of the revolutionary war.

The party that took us consisted of six Indians and four Frenchmen, who immediately commenced plundering, as I just observed, and took what they considered most valuable; consisting principally of bread, meal and meat. Having taken as much provision as they could carry, they set out with their prisoners in great haste, for fear of detection, and soon entered the woods. On our march that day, an Indian went behind us with a whip, with which he frequently lashed the children to make them keep up. In this manner we travelled till dark without a mouthful of food or a drop of water; although we had not eaten since the night before. Whenever the little children cried for water, the Indians would make them drink urine or go thirsty. At night they encamped in the woods without fire and without shelter, where we were watched with the greatest vigilance. Extremely fatigued, and very hungry, we were compelled to lie upon the ground supperless and without a drop of water to satisfy the cravings of our appetites. As in the day time, so the little ones were made to drink urine in the night if they cried for water. Fatigue alone brought us a little sleep for the refreshment of our weary limbs; and at the dawn of day we were again started on our march in the same order that we had proceeded on the day before. About sunrise we were halted, and the Indians gave us a full breakfast of provision that they had brought from my father's house. Each of us being very hungry, partook of this bounty of the Indians, except father, who was so much overcome with his situation—so much exhausted by anxiety and grief, that silent despair seemed fastened upon his countenance, and he could not be prevailed upon to refresh his sinking nature by the use of a morsel of food. Our repast being finished, we again resumed our march, and before noon passed a small fort that I heard my father say was called Fort Canagojigge.

That was the only time that I heard him speak from the time we were taken till we were finally separated the following night.

Towards evening we arrived at the border of a dark and dismal swamp, which was covered with small hemlocks, or some other evergreen, and other bushes, into which we were conducted; and having gone a short distance we stopped to encamp for the night.

Here we had some bread and meat for supper: but the dreariness of our situation, together with the uncertainty under which we all labored, as to our future destiny, almost deprived us of the sense of hunger, and destroyed our relish for food.

Mother, from the time we were taken, had manifested a great degree of fortitude, and encouraged us to support our troubles without complaining; and by her conversation seemed to make the distance and time shorter, and the way more smooth. But father lost all his ambition in the beginning of our trouble, and continued apparently lost to every care—absorbed in melancholy. Here, as before, she insisted on the necessity of our eating; and we obeyed her, but it was done with heavy hearts.

As soon as I had finished my supper, an Indian took off my shoes and stockings and put a pair of moccasins on my feet, which my mother observed; and believing that they would spare my life, even if they should destroy the other captives, addressed me as near as I can remember in the following words:—

"My dear little Mary, I fear that the time has arrived when we must be parted forever. Your life, my child, I think will be spared; but we shall probably be tomahawked here in this lonesome place by the Indians. O! how can I part with you my darling? What will become of my sweet little Mary? Oh! how can I think of your being continued in captivity without a hope of your being rescued? O that death had snatched you from my embraces in your infancy; the pain of parting then would have been pleasing to what it now is; and I should have seen the end of your troubles!—Alas, my dear! my heart bleeds at the thoughts of what awaits you; but, if you leave us, remember my child your own name, and the name of your father and mother. Be careful and not forget your English tongue. If you shall have an opportunity to get away from the Indians, don't try to escape; for if you do they will find and destroy you. Don't forget, my little daughter, the prayers that I have learned you—say them often; be a good child, and God will bless you. May God bless you my child, and make you comfortable and happy."

During this time, the Indians stripped the shoes and stockings from the little boy that belonged to the woman who was taken with us, and put moccasins on his feet, as they had done before on mine. I was crying. An Indian took the little boy and myself by the hand, to lead us off from the company, when my mother exclaimed, "Don't cry Mary—don't cry my child. God will bless you! Farewell—farewell!"

The Indian led us some distance into the bushes, or woods, and there lay down with us to spend the night. The recollection of parting with my tender mother kept me awake, while the tears constantly flowed from my eyes. A number of times in the night the little boy begged of me earnestly to run away with him and get clear of the Indians; but remembering the advice I had so lately received, and knowing the dangers to which we should be exposed, in travelling without a path and without a guide, through a wilderness unknown to us, I told him that I would not go, and persuaded him to lie still till morning.

Early the next morning the Indians and Frenchmen that we had left the night before, came to us; but our friends were left behind. It is impossible for any one to form a correct idea of what my feelings were at the sight of those savages, whom I supposed had murdered my parents and brothers, sister, and friends, and left them in the swamp to be devoured by wild beasts! But what could I do? A poor little defenceless girl; without the power or means of escaping; without a home to go to, even if I could be liberated; without a knowledge of the direction or distance to my former place of residence; and without a living friend to whom to fly for protection, I felt a kind of horror, anxiety, and dread, that, to me, seemed insupportable. I durst not cry—I durst not complain; and to inquire of them the fate of my friends (even if I could have mustered resolution) was beyond my ability, as I could not speak their language, nor they understand mine. My only relief was in silent stifled sobs.

My suspicions as to the fate of my parents proved too true; for soon after I left them they were killed and scalped, together with Robert, Matthew, Betsey, and the woman and her two children, and mangled in the most shocking manner.

Having given the little boy and myself some bread and meat for breakfast, they led us on as fast as we could travel, and one of them went behind and with a long staff, picked up all the grass and weeds that we trailed down by going over them. By taking that precaution they avoided detection; for each weed was so nicely placed in its natural position that no one would have suspected that we had passed that way. It is the custom of Indians when scouting, or on private expeditions, to step carefully and where no impression of their feet can be left—shunning wet or muddy ground. They seldom take hold of a bush or limb, and never break one; and by observing those precautions and that of setting up the weeds and grass which they necessarily lop, they completely elude the sagacity of their pursuers, and escape that punishment which they are conscious they merit from the hand of justice.

After a hard day's march we encamped in a thicket, where the Indians made a shelter of boughs, and then built a good fire to warm and dry our benumbed limbs and clothing; for it had rained some through the day. Here we were again fed as before. When the Indians had finished their supper they took from their baggage a number of scalps and went about preparing them for the market, or to keep without spoiling, by straining them over small hoops which they prepared for that purpose, and then drying and scraping them by the fire. Having put the scalps, yet wet and bloody, upon the hoops, and stretched them to their full extent, they held them to the fire till they were partly dried and then with their knives commenced scraping off the flesh; and in that way they continued to work, alternately drying and scraping them, till they were dry and clean. That being done they combed the hair in the neatest manner, and then painted it and the edges of the scalps yet on the hoops, red. Those scalps I knew at the time must have been taken from our family by the color of the hair. My mother's hair was red; and I could easily distinguish my father's and the children's from each other. That sight was most appaling; yet, I was obliged to endure it without complaining.

In the course of the night they made me to understand that they should not have killed the family if the whites had not pursued them.

Mr. Fields, whom I have before mentioned, informed me that at the time we were taken, he lived in the vicinity of my father; and that on hearing of our captivity, the whole neighborhood turned out in pursuit of the enemy, and to deliver us if possible: but that their efforts were unavailing. They however pursued us to the dark swamp, where they found my father, his family and companions, stripped and mangled in the most inhuman manner: That from thence the march of the cruel monsters could not be traced in any direction; and that they returned to their homes with the melancholy tidings of our misfortunes, supposing that we had all shared in the massacre.

The next morning we went on; the Indian going behind us and setting up the weeds as on the day before. At night we encamped on the ground in the open air, without a shelter or fire.

In the morning we again set out early, and travelled as on the two former days, though the weather was extremely uncomfortable, from the continual falling of rain and snow.

At night the snow fell fast, and the Indians built a shelter of boughs, and a fire, where we rested tolerably dry through that and the two succeeding nights.

When we stopped, and before the fire was kindled, I was so much fatigued from running, and so far benumbed by the wet and cold, that I expected that I must fail and die before I could get warm and comfortable. The fire, however, soon restored the circulation, and after I had taken my supper I felt so that I rested well through the night.

On account of the storm, we were two days at that place. On one of those days, a party consisting of six Indians who had been to the frontier settlements, came to where we were, and brought with them one prisoner, a young white man who was very tired and dejected. His name I have forgotten.

Misery certainly loves company. I was extremely glad to see him, though I knew from his appearance, that his situation was as deplorable as mine, and that he could afford me no kind of assistance. In the afternoon the Indians killed a deer, which they dressed, and then roasted it whole; which made them a full meal. We were each allowed a share of their venison, and some bread, so that we made a good meal also.

Having spent three nights and two days at that place, and the storm having ceased, early in the morning the whole company, consisting of twelve Indians, four Frenchmen, the young man, the little boy and myself, moved on at a moderate pace without an Indian behind us to deceive our pursuers.

In the afternoon we came in sight of Fort Pitt (as it is now called), where we were halted while the Indians performed some customs upon their prisoners which they deemed necessary. That fort was then occupied by the French and Indians, and was called Fort Du Quesne. It stood at the junction of the Monongahela, which is said to signify, in some of the Indian languages, the Falling-in-Banks,* and the Alleghany† rivers, where the Ohio river begins to take its name. The word O-hi-o, signifies bloody.

At the place where we halted, the Indians combed the hair of the young man, the boy and myself, and then painted our faces and hair red, in the finest Indian style. We were then conducted into the fort, where we received a little bread, and were then shut up and left to tarry alone through the night.

❖◯❖◯❖

CHAPTER III.

She is given to two Squaws. Her Journey down the Ohio. Passes a Shawanee town where white men had just been burnt. Arrives at the Seneca town. Her Reception. She is adopted. Ceremony of Adoption. Indian Custom. Address. She receives a new name. Her Employment. Retains her own and learns the Seneca Language. Situation of the Town, &c. Indians go on a Hunting Tour to Sciota and take her with them. Returns. She is taken to Fort Pitt, and then hurried back by her Indian Sisters. Her hopes of Liberty destroyed. Second Tour to Sciota. Return to Wiishto, &c. Arrival of Prisoners. Priscilla Ramsay. Her Chain. Mary marries a Delaware. Her Affection for him. Birth and Death of her first Child. Her Sickness and Recovery. Birth of Thomas Jemison.

THE night was spent in gloomy forebodings. What the result of our captivity would be, it was

*Navigator.

†The word Alleghenny, was derived from an ancient race of Indians called "Tallegawe." The Delaware Indians, instead of saying "Alleghenny," say "Allegawe," or "Allegawenink." *Western Tour—p.* 455.

out of our power to determine or even imagine.—
At times we could almost realize the approach of
our masters to butcher and scalp us;—again we
could nearly see the pile of wood kindled on which
we were to be roasted; and then we would imagine
ourselves at liberty; alone and defenceless in the
forest, surrounded by wild beasts that were ready
to devour us. The anxiety of our minds drove sleep
from our eyelids; and it was with a dreadful hope
and painful impatience that we waited for the
morning to determine our fate.

The morning at length arrived, and our masters
came early and let us out of the house, and gave the
young man and boy to the French, who immediately took them away. Their fate I never learned;
as I have not seen nor heard of them since.

I was now left alone in the fort, deprived of my
former companions, and of everything that was near
or dear to me but life. But it was not long before I
was in some measure relieved by the appearance
of two pleasant looking squaws of the Seneca tribe,
who came and examined me attentively for a short
time, and then went out. After a few minutes absence they returned with my former masters, who
gave me to them to dispose of as they pleased.

The Indians by whom I was taken were a party
of Shawanees, if I remember right, that lived,
when at home, a long distance down the Ohio.

My former Indian masters, and the two squaws,
were soon ready to leave the fort, and accordingly
embarked; the Indians in a large canoe, and the
two squaws and myself in a small one, and went
down the Ohio.

When we set off, an Indian in the forward canoe took the scalps of my former friends, strung them on a pole that he placed upon his shoulder, and in that manner carried them, standing in the stern of the canoe, directly before us as we sailed down the river, to the town where the two squaws resided.

On our way we passed a Shawanee town, where I saw a number of heads, arms, legs, and other fragments of the bodies of some white people who had just been burnt. The parts that remained were hanging on a pole which was supported at each end by a crotch stuck in the ground, and were roasted or burnt black as a coal. The fire was yet burning; and the whole appearances afforded a spectacle so shocking, that, even to this day, my blood almost curdles in my veins when I think of them!

At night we arrived at a small Seneca Indian town, at the mouth of a small river, that was called by the Indians, in the Seneca language, She-nan-jee,* where the two Squaws to whom I belonged resided. There we landed, and the Indians went on; which was the last I ever saw of them.

Having made fast to the shore, the Squaws left me in the canoe while they went to their wigwam or house in the town, and returned with a suit of Indian clothing, all new, and very clean and nice. My clothes, though whole and good when I was

*That town, according to the geographical description given by Mrs. Jemison, must have stood at the mouth of Indian Cross creek, which is about 76 miles by water, below Pittsburgh; or at the mouth of Indian Short creek, 87 miles below Pittsburgh, where the town of Warren now stands. But at which of those places I am unable to determine. *Author.*

taken, were now torn in pieces, so that I was almost naked. They first undressed me and threw my rags into the river; then washed me clean and dressed me in the new suit they had just brought, in complete Indian style; and then led me home and seated me in the center of their wigwam.

I had been in that situation but a few minutes, before all the Squaws in the town came in to see me. I was soon surrounded by them, and they immediately set up a most dismal howling, crying bitterly, and wringing their hands in all the agonies of grief for a deceased relative.

Their tears flowed freely, and they exhibited all the signs of real mourning. At the commencement of this scene, one of their number began, in a voice somewhat between speaking and singing, to recite some words to the following purport, and continued the recitation till the ceremony was ended; the company at the same time varying the appearance of their countenances, gestures and tone of voice, so as to correspond with the sentiments expressed by their leader:

"Oh our brother! Alas! He is dead—he has gone; he will never return! Friendless he died on the field of the slain, where his bones are yet lying unburied! Oh, who will not mourn his sad fate? No tears dropped around him; oh, no! No tears of his sisters were there! He fell in his prime, when his arm was most needed to keep us from danger! Alas! he has gone! and left us in sorrow, his loss to bewail: Oh where is his spirit? His spirit went naked, and hungry it wanders, and thirsty and wounded it groans to return! Oh helpless and

wretched, our brother has gone! No blanket nor
food to nourish and warm him; nor candles to
light him, nor weapons of war:—Oh, none of those
comforts had he! But well we remember his deeds!
—The deer he could take on the chase! The panther shrunk back at the sight of his strength! His
enemies fell at his feet! He was brave and courageous in war! As the fawn he was harmless: his
friendship was ardent: his temper was gentle: his
pity was great! Oh! our friend, our companion is
dead! Our brother, our brother, alas! he is gone!
But why do we grieve for his loss? In the strength
of a warrior, undaunted he left us, to fight by the
side of the Chiefs! His war-whoop was shrill! His
rifle well aimed laid his enemies low: his tomahawk drank of their blood: and his knife flayed
their scalps while yet covered with gore! And why
do we mourn? Though he fell on the field of the
slain, with glory he fell, and his spirit went up to
the land of his fathers in war! Then why do we
mourn? With transports of joy they received him,
and fed him, and clothed him, and welcomed him
there! Oh friends, he is happy; then dry up your
tears! His spirit has seen our distress, and sent us
a helper whom with pleasure we greet. Dickewamis
has come: then let us receive her with joy! She is
handsome and pleasant! Oh! she is our sister, and
gladly we welcome her here. In the place of our
brother she stands in our tribe. With care we will
guard her from trouble; and may she be happy till
her spirit shall leave us."

In the course of that ceremony, from mourning they became serene — joy sparkled in their

countenances, and they seemed to rejoice over me as over a long lost child. I was made welcome amongst them as a sister to the two Squaws before mentioned, and was called Dickewamis; which being interpreted, signifies a pretty girl, a handsome girl, or a pleasant, good thing. That is the name by which I have ever since been called by the Indians.

I afterwards learned that the ceremony I at that time passed through, was that of adoption. The two squaws had lost a brother in Washington's war, sometime in the year before, and in consequence of his death went up to Fort Pitt, on the day on which I arrived there, in order to receive a prisoner or an enemy's scalp, to supply their loss.

It is a custom of the Indians, when one of their number is slain or taken prisoner in battle, to give to the nearest relative to the dead or absent, a prisoner, if they have chanced to take one, and if not, to give him the scalp of an enemy. On the return of the Indians from conquest, which is always announced by peculiar shoutings, demonstrations of joy, and the exhibition of some trophy of victory, the mourners come forward and make their claims. If they receive a prisoner, it is at their option either to satiate their vengeance by taking his life in the most cruel manner they can conceive of; or, to receive and adopt him into the family, in the place of him whom they have lost. All the prisoners that are taken in battle and carried to the encampment or town by the Indians, are given to the bereaved families, till their number is made good. And unless the mourners have but just received the news of their bereavement, and are under the operation of a paroxysm of grief, anger and revenge; or, unless the prisoner is very old, sickly, or homely, they generally save him, and treat him kindly. But if their mental wound is fresh, their loss so great that they deem it irreparable, or if their prisoner or prisoners do not meet their approbation, no torture, let it be ever so cruel, seems sufficient to make them satisfaction. It is family, and not national, sacrifices amongst the Indians, that has given them an indelible stamp as barbarians, and identified their character with the idea which is generally formed of unfeeling ferocity, and the most abandoned cruelty.

It was my happy lot to be accepted for adoption; and at the time of the ceremony I was received by the two squaws, to supply the place of their brother in the family; and I was ever considered and treated by them as a real sister, the same as though I had been born of their mother.

During my adoption, I sat motionless, nearly terrified to death at the appearance and actions of the company, expecting every moment to feel their vengeance, and suffer death on the spot. I was, however, happily disappointed, when at the close of the ceremony the company retired, and my sisters went about employing every means for my consolation and comfort.

Being now settled and provided with a home, I was employed in nursing the children, and doing light work about the house. Occasionally I was sent out with the Indian hunters, when they went but a short distance, to help them carry their game. My situation was easy; I had no particular hardships to endure. But still, the recollection of my parents, my brothers and sisters, my home, and my own captivity, destroyed my happiness, and made me constantly solitary, lonesome and gloomy.

My sisters would not allow me to speak English in their hearing; but remembering the charge that my dear mother gave me at the time I left her, whenever I chanced to be alone I made a business of repeating my prayer, catechism, or something I had learned in order that I might not forget my own language. By practising in that way I retained it till I came to Genesee flats, where I soon became acquainted with English people with whom I have been almost daily in the habit of conversing.

My sisters were diligent in teaching me their language; and to their great satisfaction I soon learned so that I could understand it readily, and speak it fluently. I was very fortunate in falling into their hands; for they were kind good natured women; peaceable and mild in their dispositions; temperate and decent in their habits, and very tender and gentle towards me. I have great reason to respect them, though they have been dead a great number of years.

The town where they lived was pleasantly situated on the Ohio, at the mouth of the Shenanjee: the land produced good corn; the woods furnished a plenty of game, and the waters abounded with fish. Another river emptied itself into the Ohio, directly opposite the mouth of the Shenanjee. We spent the summer at that place, where we planted, hoed, and harvested a large crop of corn, of an excellent quality.

About the time of corn harvest, Fort Pitt was taken from the French by the English.*

The corn being harvested, the Indians took it on horses and in canoes, and proceeded down the Ohio, occasionally stopping to hunt a few days, till we arrived at the mouth of Sciota river; where they established their winter quarters, and continued hunting till the ensuing spring, in the adjacent wilderness. While at that place I went with the other children to assist the hunters to bring in their game. The forests on the Sciota were well stocked with elk, deer, and other large animals; and the marshes contained large numbers of beaver, muskrat, &c. which made excellent hunting for the Indians; who depended, for their meat, upon their success in taking elk and deer; and for ammunition and clothing, upon the beaver, muskrat, and other furs that they could take in addition to their peltry.

The season for hunting being passed, we all returned in the spring to the mouth of the river Shenanjee, to the houses and fields we had left in

*The above statement is apparently an error; and is to be attributed solely to the treachery of the old lady's memory; though she is confident that that event took place at the time above mentioned. It is certain that Fort Pitt was not evacuated by the French and given up to the English, till sometime in November, 1758. It is possible, however, that an armistice was agreed upon, and that for a time, between the spring of 1755 and 1758, both nations visited that post without fear of molestation. As the succeeding part of the narrative corresponds with the true historical chain of events, the public will overlook this circumstance, which appears unsupported by history.   AUTHOR.

the fall before. There we again planted our corn, squashes, and beans, on the fields that we occupied the preceding summer.

About planting time, our Indians all went up to Fort Pitt, to make peace with the British, and took me with them.* We landed on the opposite side of the river from the fort, and encamped for the night. Early the next morning the Indians took me over to the fort to see the white people that were there. It was then that my heart bounded to be liberated from the Indians and to be restored to my friends and my country. The white people were surprized to see me with the Indians, enduring the hardships of a savage life, at so early an age, and with so delicate a constitution as I appeared to possess. They asked me my name; where and when I was taken—and appeared very much interested on my behalf. They were continuing their inquiries, when my sisters became alarmed, believing that I should be taken from them, hurried me into their canoe and recrossed the river— took their bread out of the fire and fled with me, without stopping, till they arrived at the river Shenanjee. So great was their fear of losing me, or of my being given up in the treaty, that they never once stopped rowing till they got home.

Shortly after we left the shore opposite the fort, as I was informed by one of my Indian brothers,

*History is silent as to any treaty having been made between the English, and French and Indians, at that time; though it is possible that a truce was agreed upon, and that the parties met for the purpose of concluding a treaty of peace.

the white people came over to take me back; but after considerable inquiry, and having made diligent search to find where I was hid, they returned with heavy hearts. Although I had then been with the Indians something over a year, and had become considerably habituated to their mode of living, and attached to my sisters, the sight of white people who could speak English inspired me with an unspeakable anxiety to go home with them, and share in the blessings of civilization. My sudden departure and escape from them, seemed like a second captivity, and for a long time I brooded the thoughts of my miserable situation with almost as much sorrow and dejection as I had done those of my first sufferings. Time, the destroyer of every affection, wore away my unpleasant feelings, and I became as contented as before.

We tended our cornfields through the summer; and after we had harvested the crop, we again went down the river to the hunting ground on the Sciota, where we spent the winter, as we had done the winter before.

Early in the spring we sailed up the Ohio river, to a place that the Indians called Wiishto,* where one river emptied into the Ohio on one side, and another on the other. At that place the Indians built a town, and we planted corn.

We lived three summers at Wiishto, and spent each winter on the Sciota.

*Wiishto I suppose was situated near the mouth of Indian Guyundat, 327 miles below Pittsburgh, and 73 above Big Sciota; or at the mouth of Swan creek, 307 miles below Pittsburgh.

The first summer of our living at Wiishto, a party of Delaware Indians came up the river, took up their residence, and lived in common with us. They brought five white prisoners with them, who by their conversation, made my situation much more agreeable, as they could all speak English. I have forgotten the names of all of them except one, which was Priscilla Ramsay. She was a very handsome, good natured girl, and was married soon after she came to Wiishto to Capt. Little Billy's uncle, who went with her on a visit to her friends in the states. Having tarried with them as long as she wished to, she returned with her husband to Can-a-ah-tua, where he died. She, after his death, married a white man by the name of Nettles, and now lives with him (if she is living) on Grand River, Upper Canada.

Not long after the Delawares came to live with us, at Wiishto, my sisters told me that I must go and live with one of them, whose name was Shenin-jee. Not daring to cross them, or disobey their commands, with a great degree of reluctance I went; and Sheninjee and I were married according to Indian custom.

Sheninjee was a noble man; large in stature; elegant in his appearance; generous in his conduct; courageous in war; a friend to peace, and a great lover of justice. He supported a degree of dignity far above his rank, and merited and received the confidence and friendship of all the tribes with whom he was acquainted. Yet, Sheninjee was an Indian. The idea of spending my days with him, at first seemed perfectly irreconcilable to my feelings: but his good nature, generosity, tenderness, and friendship towards me, soon gained my affection; and, strange as it may seem, I loved him!— To me he was ever kind in sickness, and always treated me with gentleness; in fact, he was an agreeable husband, and a comfortable companion. We lived happily together till the time of our final separation, which happened two or three years after our marriage, as I shall presently relate.

In the second summer of my living at Wiishto, I had a child at the time that the kernels of corn first appeared on the cob. When I was taken sick, Sheninjee was absent, and I was sent to a small shed, on the bank of the river, which was made of boughs, where I was obliged to stay till my husband returned. My two sisters, who were my only companions, attended me, and on the second day of my confinement my child was born; but it lived only two days. It was a girl: and notwithstanding the shortness of the time that I possessed it, it was a great grief to me to lose it.

After the birth of my child, I was very sick, but was not allowed to go into the house for two weeks; when, to my great joy, Sheninjee returned, and I was taken in and as comfortably provided for as our situation would admit of. My disease continued to increase for a number of days; and I became so far reduced that my recovery was despaired of by my friends, and I concluded that my troubles would soon be finished. At length, however, my complaint took a favorable turn, and by the time that the corn was ripe I was able to get about. I continued to gain my health, and in the fall was able to go to our winter quarters, on the Sciota, with the Indians.

From that time, nothing remarkable occurred to me till the fourth winter of my captivity, when I had a son born, while I was at Sciota: I had a quick recovery, and my child was healthy. To commemorate the name of my much lamented father, I called my son Thomas Jemison.

❖◉❖◉❖

CHAPTER IV.

She leaves Wiishto for Fort Pitt, in company with her Husband. Her feelings on setting out. Contrast between the labor of the white and Indian Women. Deficiency of Arts amongst the Indians. Their former Happiness. Baneful effects of Civilization, and the introduction of ardent Spirits amongst them, &c. Journey up the River. Murder of three Traders by the Shawnees. Her Husband stops at a Trading House. Wantonness of the Shawnees. Moves up the Sandusky. Meets her Brother from Ge-nish-a-u. Her Husband goes to Wiishto, and she sets out for Genishau in company with her Brothers. They arrive at Sandusky. Occurrences at that place. Her Journey to Genishau, and Reception by her Mother and Friends.

IN the spring, when Thomas was three or four moons [months] old, we returned from Sciota to Wiishto, and soon after set out to go to Fort Pitt, to dispose of our fur and skins, that we had taken in the winter, and procure some necessary articles for the use of our family.

I had then been with the Indians four summers and four winters, and had become so far accustomed to their mode of living, habits and dispositions, that my anxiety to get away, to be set at liberty, and leave them, had almost subsided. With them was my home; my family was there, and there I had many friends to whom I was warmly attached in consideration of the favors, affection and friendship with which they had uniformly treated me, from the time of my adoption. Our labor was not severe; and that of one year was exactly similar, in almost every respect, to that of the others, without that endless variety that is to be observed in the common labor of the white people. Notwithstanding the Indian women have all the fuel and bread to procure, and the cooking to perform, their task is probably not harder than that of white women, who have those articles provided for them; and their cares certainly are not half as numerous, nor as great. In the summer season, we planted, tended and harvested our corn, and generally had all our children with us; but had no master to oversee or drive us, so that we could work as leisurely as we pleased. We had no ploughs on the Ohio; but performed the whole process of planting and hoeing with a small tool that resembled, in some respects, a hoe with a very short handle.

Our cooking consisted in pounding our corn into samp or hommany, boiling the hommany, making now and then a cake and baking it in the ashes, and in boiling or roasting our venison. As our cooking and eating utensils consisted of a hommany block and pestle, a small kettle, a knife or two, and a few vessels of bark or wood, it required but little time to keep them in order for use.

Spinning, weaving, sewing, stocking knitting,

and the like, are arts which have never been practised in the Indian tribes generally. After the revolutionary war, I learned to sew, so that I could make my own clothing after a poor fashion; but the other domestic arts I have been wholly ignorant of the application of, since my captivity. In the season of hunting, it was our business, in addition to our cooking, to bring home the game that was taken by the Indians, dress it, and carefully preserve the eatable meat, and prepare or dress the skins. Our clothing was fastened together with strings of deer skin, and tied on with the same.

In that manner we lived, without any of those jealousies, quarrels, and revengeful battles between families and individuals, which have been common in the Indian tribes since the introduction of ardent spirits amongst them.

The use of ardent spirits amongst the Indians, and the attempts which have been made to civilize and christianize them by the white people, has constantly made them worse and worse; increased their vices, and robbed them of many of their virtues; and will ultimately produce their extermination. I have seen, in a number of instances, the effects of education upon some of our Indians, who were taken when young, from their families, and placed at school before they had had an opportunity to contract many Indian habits, and there kept till they arrived to manhood; but I have never seen one of those but what was an Indian in every respect after he returned. Indians must and will be Indians, in spite of all the means that can be used for their cultivation in the sciences and arts.

One thing only marred my happiness, while I lived with them on the Ohio; and that was the recollection that I had once had tender parents, and a home that I loved. Aside from that consideration, or, if I had been taken in infancy, I should have been contented in my situation. Notwithstanding all that has been said against the Indians, in consequence of their cruelties to their enemies—cruelties that I have witnessed, and had abundant proof of—it is a fact that they are naturally kind, tender and peaceable towards their friends, and strictly honest; and that those cruelties have been practised, only upon their enemies, according to their idea of justice.

At the time we left Wiishto, it was impossible for me to suppress a sigh of regret on parting with those who had truly been my friends—with those whom I had every reason to respect. On account of a part of our family living at Genishau, we thought it doubtful whether we should return directly from Pittsburgh, or go from thence on a visit to see them.

Our company consisted of my husband, my two Indian brothers, my little son and myself. We embarked in a canoe that was large enough to contain ourselves and our effects, and proceeded on our voyage up the river.

Nothing remarkable occurred to us on our way, till we arrived at the mouth of a creek which Sheninjee and my brothers said was the outlet of Sandusky lake; where, as they said, two or three English traders in fur and skins had kept a trading house but a short time before, though they were then absent. We had passed the trading house but a short distance, when we met three white men floating down the river, with the appearance of having been recently murdered by the Indians. We supposed them to be the bodies of the traders, whose store we had passed the same day. Sheninjee being alarmed for fear of being apprehended as one of the murderers, if he should go on, resolved to put about immediately, and we accordingly returned to where the traders had lived, and there landed.

At the trading house we found a party of Shawnee Indians, who had taken a young white man prisoner, and had just begun to torture him for the sole purpose of gratifying their curiosity in exulting at his distress. They at first made him stand up, while they slowly pared his ears and split them into strings; they then made a number of slight incisions in his face; and then bound him upon the ground, rolled him in the dirt, and rubbed it in his wounds: some of them at the same time whipping him with small rods! The poor fellow cried for mercy and yelled most piteously.

The sight of his distress seemed too much for me to endure: I begged of them to desist—I entreated them with tears to release him. At length they attended to my intercessions, and set him at liberty. He was shockingly disfigured, bled profusely, and appeared to be in great pain: but as soon as he was liberated he made off in haste, which was the last I saw of him.

We soon learned that the same party of Shawnees had, but a few hours before, massacred the three white traders whom we saw in the river, and had plundered their store. We, however, were not molested by them, and after a short stay at that place, moved up the creek about forty miles to a Shawnee town, which the Indians called Gawgush-shaw-ga, (which being interpreted signifies a mask or a false face.) The creek that we went up was called Candusky.

It was now summer; and having tarried a few days at Gawgushshawga, we moved on up the creek to a place that was called Yis-kah-wa-na, (meaning in English open mouth.)

As I have before observed, the family to which I belonged was part of a tribe of Seneca Indians, who lived, at that time, at a place called Genishau, from the name of the tribe, that was situated on a river of the same name which is now called Genesee. The word Genishau signifies a shining, clear or open place. Those of us who lived on the Ohio, had frequently received invitations from those at Genishau, by one of my brothers, who usually went and returned every season, to come and live with them, and my two sisters had been gone almost two years.

While we were at Yiskahwana, my brother arrived there from Genishau, and insisted so strenuously upon our going home (as he called it) with him, that my two brothers concluded to go, and to take me with them.

By this time the summer was gone, and the time for harvesting corn had arrived. My brothers, for fear of the rainy season setting in early, thought it best to set out immediately that we might have good travelling. Sheninjee consented to have me go with my brothers; but concluded to go down the river himself with some fur and skins which he had on hand, spend the winter in hunting with his friends, and come to me in the spring following.

That was accordingly agreed upon, and he set out for Wiishto; and my three brothers and myself, with my little son on my back, at the same time set out for Genishau. We came on to Upper Sandusky, to an Indian town that we found deserted by its inhabitants, in consequence of their having recently murdered some English traders, who resided amongst them. That town was owned and had been occupied by Delaware Indians, who, when they left it, buried their provision in the earth, in order to preserve it from their enemies, or to have a supply for themselves if they should chance to return. My brothers understood the customs of the Indians when they were obliged to fly from their enemies; and suspecting that their corn at least must have been hid, made diligent search, and at length found a large quantity of it, together with beans, sugar and honey, so carefully buried that it was completely dry and as good as when they left it. As our stock of provision was scanty, we considered ourselves extremely fortunate in finding so seasonable a supply, with so little trouble. Having caught two or three horses, that we found there, and furnished ourselves with a good store of food, we travelled on till we came to the mouth of French Creek, where we hunted two days, and from thence came on to Conowongo Creek, where we were obliged to stay seven or ten days, in consequence of our horses having left us and straying into the woods. The horses, however, were found, and we again prepared to resume our journey. During our stay at that place the rain fell fast, and had raised the creek to such a height that it was seemingly impossible for us to cross it. A number of times we ventured in, but were compelled to return, barely escaping with our lives. At length we succeeded in swimming our horses and reached the opposite shore; though I but just escaped with my little boy from being drowned. From Sandusky the path that we travelled was crooked and obscure; but was tolerably well understood by my oldest brother, who had travelled it a number of times, when going to and returning from the Cherokee wars. The fall by this time was considerably advanced, and the rains, attended with cold winds, continued daily to increase the difficulties of travelling. From Conowongo we came to a place, called by the Indians Che-ua-shung-gau-tau, and from that to U-na-waum-gwa, (which means an eddy, not strong,) where the early frosts had destroyed the corn so that the Indians were in danger of starving for the want of bread. Having rested ourselves two days at that place, we came on to Caneadea and stayed one day, and then continued our march till we arrived at Geni-shau. Genishau at that time was a large Seneca town, thickly inhabited, lying on Genesee river, opposite what is now called the Free Ferry, adjoining Fall-Brook, and about south west of the present village of Geneseo, the county seat for the county of Livingston, in the state of New-York.

Those only who have travelled on foot the distance of five or six hundred miles, through an almost pathless wilderness, can form an idea of the fatigue and sufferings that I endured on that journey. My clothing was thin and illy calculated to defend me from the continually drenching rains with which I was daily completely wet, and at night with nothing but my wet blanket to cover me, I had to sleep on the naked ground, and generally without a shelter, save such as nature had provided. In addition to all that, I had to carry my child, then about nine months old, every step of the journey on my back, or in my arms, and provide for his comfort and prevent his suffering, as far as my poverty of means would admit. Such was the fatigue that I sometimes felt, that I thought it impossible for me to go through, and I would almost abandon the idea of even trying to proceed. My brothers were attentive, and at length, as I have stated, we reached our place of destination, in good health, and without having experienced a day's sickness from the time we left Yiskahwana.

We were kindly received by my Indian mother and the other members of the family, who appeared to make me welcome; and my two sisters, whom I had not seen in two years, received me with every expression of love and friendship, and that they really felt what they expressed, I have never had the least reason to doubt. The warmth of their feelings, the kind reception which I met with, and the continued favors that I received at their hands, rivetted my affection for them so strongly that I am constrained to believe that I loved them as I should have loved my own sister had she lived, and I had been brought up with her.

✥◉✥◉✥

CHAPTER V.

Indians march to Niagara to fight the British. Return with two Prisoners, &c. Sacrifice them at Fall-Brook. Her Indian Mother's Address to her Daughter. Death of her Husband. Bounty offered for the Prisoners taken in the last war. John Van Sice attempts to take her to procure her Ransom. Her Escape. Edict of the Chiefs. Old King of the tribe determines to have her given up. Her brother threatens her Life. Her narrow Escape. The old King goes off. Her brother is informed of the place of her concealment, and conducts her home. Marriage to her second Husband. Names of her Children.

WHEN we arrived at Genishau, the Indians of that tribe were making active preparations for joining the French, in order to assist them in retaking Fort Ne-a-gaw (as Fort Niagara was called in the Seneca language) from the British, who had taken it from the French in the month preceding. They marched off the next day after our arrival, painted and accoutred in all the habiliments of Indian warfare, determined on death or victory; and joined the army in season to assist in accomplishing a plan that had been previously concerted for the destruction of a part of the British army. The British feeling themselves secure in the possession of Fort Neagaw, and unwilling that their enemies should occupy any of the military posts in that quarter, determined to take Fort Schlosser, lying a few miles up the river from Neagaw, which they expected to effect with but little loss. Accordingly a detachment of soldiers, sufficiently numerous, as was supposed, was sent out to take it, leaving a strong garrison in the fort, and marched off, well prepared to effect their object. But on their way they were surrounded by the French and Indians, who lay in ambush to receive them, and were driven off the bank of the river into a place called the "Devil's Hole," together with their horses, carriages, artillery, and every thing pertaining to the army. Not a single man escaped being driven off, and of the whole number one only was fortunate enough to escape with his life.* Our Indians were absent but a few days, and returned in triumph, bringing with them two white prisoners, and a number of oxen. Those were the first neat cattle that were ever brought to the Genesee flats.

The next day after their return to Genishau, was set apart as a day of feasting and frolicing, at the expence of the lives of their two unfortunate prisoners, on whom they purposed to glut their revenge, and satisfy their love for retaliation upon their enemies. My sister was anxious to attend the execution, and to take me with her, to witness the customs of the warriors, as it was one of the highest kind of frolics ever celebrated in their tribe, and one that was not often attended with so much pomp and parade as it was expected that would be. I felt a kind of anxiety to witness the scene, having never attended an execution, and yet I felt a kind of horrid dread that made my heart revolt, and inclined me to step back rather than support

*For the particulars of that event, see Appendix, No. 1.

the idea of advancing. On the morning of the execution she made her intention of going to the frolic, and taking me with her, known to our mother, who in the most feeling terms remonstrated against a step at once so rash and unbecoming the true dignity of our sex:

"How, my daughter, (said she, addressing my sister,) how can you even think of attending the feast and seeing the unspeakable torments that those poor unfortunate prisoners must inevitably suffer from the hands of our warriors? How can you stand and see them writhing in the warriors' fire, in all the agonies of a slow, a lingering death? How can you think of enduring the sound of their groanings and prayers to the Great Spirit for sudden deliverance from their enemies, or from life? And how can you think of conducting to that melancholy spot your poor sister Dickewamis, (meaning myself,) who has so lately been a prisoner, who has lost her parents and brothers by the hands of the bloody warriors, and who has felt all the horrors of the loss of her freedom, in lonesome captivity? Oh! how can you think of making her bleed at the wounds which now are but partially healed? The recollection of her former troubles would deprive us of Dickewamis, and she would depart to the fields of the blessed, where fighting has ceased, and the corn needs no tending—where hunting is easy, the forests delightful, the summers are pleasant, and the winters are mild!—O! think once, my daughter, how soon you may have a brave brother made prisoner in battle, and sacrificed to feast the ambition of the enemies of his kindred, and leave us to mourn for the loss of a friend, a son and a brother, whose bow brought us venison, and supplied us with blankets!—Our task is quite easy at home, and our business needs our attention. With war we have nothing to do: our husbands and brothers are proud to defend us, and their hearts beat with ardor to meet our proud foes. Oh! stay then, my daughter; let our warriors alone perform on their victims their customs of war!"

This speech of our mother had the desired effect; we stayed at home and attended to our domestic concerns. The prisoners, however, were executed by having their heads taken off, their bodies cut in pieces and shockingly mangled, and then burnt to ashes!—They were burnt on the north side of Fall-brook, directly opposite the town which was on the south side, some time in the month of November, 1759.

I spent the winter comfortably, and as agreeably as I could have expected to, in the absence of my kind husband. Spring at length appeared, but Sheninjee was yet away; summer came on, but my husband had not found me. Fearful forebodings haunted my imagination; yet I felt confident that his affection for me was so great that if he was alive he would follow me and I should again see him. In the course of the summer, however, I received intelligence that soon after he left me at Yiskahwana he was taken sick and died at Wiishto. This was a heavy and an unexpected blow. I was now in my youthful days left a widow, with one son, and entirely dependent on myself for his and my support. My mother and her family gave me all the consolation in their power, and in a few months my grief wore off and I became contented.

In a year or two after this, according to my best recollection of the time, the King of England offered a bounty to those who would bring in the prisoners that had been taken in the war, to some military post where they might be redeemed and set at liberty.

John Van Sice, a Dutchman, who had frequently been at our place, and was well acquainted with every prisoner at Genishau, resolved to take me to Niagara, that I might there receive my liberty and he the offered bounty. I was notified of his intention; but as I was fully determined not to be redeemed at that time, especially with his assistance, I carefully watched his movements in order to avoid falling into his hands. It so happened, however, that he saw me alone at work in a cornfield, and thinking probably that he could secure me easily, ran towards me in great haste. I espied him at some distance, and well knowing the amount of his errand, run from him with all the speed I was mistress of, and never once stopped till I reached Gardow.* He gave up the chase, and returned: but I, fearing that he might be lying in wait for me, stayed three days and three nights in an old cabin at Gardow, and then went back trembling at every step for fear of being apprehended. I got home without difficulty; and soon after, the chiefs in council having learned the cause of my elopement, gave orders that I should not be

*I have given this orthography, because it corresponds with the popular pronunciation.

taken to any military post without my consent;
and that as it was my choice to stay, I should live
amongst them quietly and undisturbed. But, notwithstanding the will of the chiefs, it was but a
few days before the old king of our tribe told one
of my Indian brothers that I should be redeemed,
and he would take me to Niagara himself. In reply
to the old king, my brother said that I should not
be given up; but that, as it was my wish, I should
stay with the tribe as long as I was pleased to.
Upon this a serious quarrel ensued between them,
in which my brother frankly told him that sooner
than I should be taken by force, he would kill me
with his own hands!—Highly enraged at the old
king, my brother came to my sister's house, where
I resided, and informed her of all that had passed
respecting me; and that, if the old king should attempt to take me, as he firmly believed he would,
he would immediately take my life, and hazard
the consequences. He returned to the old king. As
soon as I came in, my sister told me what she had
just heard, and what she expected without doubt
would befall me. Full of pity, and anxious for my
preservation, she then directed me to take my
child and go into some high weeds at no great distance from the house, and there hide myself and
lay still till all was silent in the house, for my
brother, she said, would return at evening and let
her know the final conclusion of the matter, of
which she promised to inform me in the following
manner: If I was to be killed, she said she would
bake a small cake and lay it at the door, on the
outside, in a place that she then pointed out to

me. When all was silent in the house, I was to creep softly to the door, and if the cake could not be found in the place specified, I was to go in: but if the cake was there, I was to take my child and go as fast as I possibly could to a large spring on the south side of Samp's Creek, (a place that I had often seen,) and there wait till I should by some means hear from her.

Alarmed for my own safety, I instantly followed her advice, and went into the weeds, where I lay in a state of the greatest anxiety, till all was silent in the house, when I crept to the door, and there found, to my great distress, the little cake! I knew my fate was fixed, unless I could keep secreted till the storm was over; and accordingly crept back to the weeds, where my little Thomas lay, took him on my back, and laid my course for the spring as fast as my legs would carry me. Thomas was nearly three years old, and very large and heavy. I got to the spring early in the morning, almost overcome with fatigue, and at the same time fearing that I might be pursued and taken, I felt my life an almost insupportable burthen. I sat down with my child at the spring, and he and I made a breakfast of the little cake, and water of the spring, which I dipped and supped with the only implement which I possessed, my hand.

In the morning after I fled, as was expected, the old King came to our house in search of me, and to take me off; but, as I was not to be found, he gave me up, and went to Niagara with the prisoners he had already got into his possession. As soon as the old King was fairly out of the way, my sister told my brother where he could find me. He immediately set out for the spring, and found me about noon. The first sight of him made me tremble with the fear of death; but when he came near, so that I could discover his countenance, tears of joy flowed down my cheeks, and I felt such a kind of instant relief as no one can possibly experience, unless when under the absolute sentence of death he receives an unlimited pardon. We were both rejoiced at the event of the old King's project; and after staying at the spring through the night, set out together for home early in the morning. When we got to a cornfield near the town, my brother secreted me till he could go and ascertain how my case stood; and finding that the old King was absent, and that all was peaceable, he returned to me, and I went home joyfully.

Not long after this, my mother went to Johnstown, on the Mohawk river, with five prisoners, who were redeemed by Sir William Johnson, and set at liberty.

When my son Thomas was three or four years old, I was married to an Indian, whose name was Hiokatoo, commonly called Gardow, by whom I had four daughters and two sons. I named my children, principally, after my relatives, from whom I was parted, by calling my girls Jane, Nancy, Betsey and Polly, and the boys John and Jesse. Jane died about twenty-nine years ago, in the month of August, a little before the great Council at Big-Tree, aged about fifteen years. My other daughters are yet living, and have families.

CHAPTER VI.

Peace amongst the Indians. Celebrations. Worship. Exercises. Business of the Tribes. Former Happiness of the Indians in time of peace extolled. Their Morals; Fidelity; Honesty; Chastity; Temperance. Indians called to German Flats. Treaty with Americans. They are sent for by the British Commissioners, and go to Oswego. Promises made by those Commissioners. Greatness of the King of England. Reward that was paid them for joining the British. They make a Treaty. Bounty offered for Scalps. Return richly dressed and equipped. In 1776 they kill a man at Cautega to provoke the Americans. Prisoners taken at Cherry Valley, brought to Beard's-Town; redeemed, &c. Battle at Fort Stanwix. Indians suffer a great loss. Mourning at Beard's Town. Mrs. Jemison's care of and services rendered to Butler and Brandt.

AFTER the conclusion of the French war, our tribe had nothing to trouble it till the commencement of the Revolution. For twelve or fifteen years the use of the implements of war was not known, nor the war-whoop heard, save on days of festivity, when the achievements of former times were commemorated in a kind of mimic warfare, in which the chiefs and warriors displayed their prowess, and illustrated their former adroitness, by laying the ambuscade, surprizing their enemies, and performing many accurate manœuvres with the tomahawk and scalping knife; thereby preserving and handing to their children, the theory of Indian warfare. During that period they also pertinaciously observed the religious rites of their progenitors, by attending with the most scrupulous exactness and a great degree of enthusiasm to the

[47]

sacrifices, at particular times, to appease the anger of the evil deity, or to excite the commisseration and friendship of the Great Good Spirit, whom they adored with reverence, as the author, governor, supporter and disposer of every good thing of which they participated.

They also practised in various athletic games, such as running, wrestling, leaping, and playing ball, with a view that their bodies might be more supple, or rather that they might not become enervated, and that they might be enabled to make a proper selection of Chiefs for the councils of the nation and leaders for war.

While the Indians were thus engaged in their round of traditionary performances, with the addition of hunting, their women attended to agriculture, their families, and a few domestic concerns of small consequence, and attended with but little labor.

No people can live more happy than the Indians did in times of peace, before the introduction of spirituous liquors amongst them. Their lives were a continual round of pleasures. Their wants were few, and easily satisfied; and their cares were only for to-day; the bounds of their calculations for future comfort not extending to the incalculable uncertainties of to-morrow. If peace ever dwelt with men, it was in former times, in the recesses from war, amongst what are now termed barbarians. The moral character of the Indians was (if I may be allowed the expression) uncontaminated. Their fidelity was perfect, and became proverbial; they were strictly honest; they despised deception and falsehood; and chastity was held in high veneration, and a violation of it was considered sacrilege. They were temperate in their desires, moderate in their passions, and candid and honorable in the expression of their sentiments on every subject of importance.

Thus, at peace amongst themselves, and with the neighboring whites, though there were none at that time very near, our Indians lived quietly and peaceably at home, till a little before the breaking out of the revolutionary war, when they were sent for, together with the Chiefs and members of the Six Nations generally, by the people of the States, to go to the German Flats, and there hold a general council, in order that the people of the states might ascertain, in good season, who they should esteem and treat as enemies, and who as friends, in the great war which was then upon the point of breaking out between them and the King of England.

Our Indians obeyed the call, and the council was holden, at which the pipe of peace was smoked, and a treaty made, in which the Six Nations solemnly agreed that if a war should eventually break out, they would not take up arms on either side; but that they would observe a strict neutrality. With that the people of the states were satisfied, as they had not asked their assistance, nor did not wish it. The Indians returned to their homes well pleased that they could live on neutral ground, surrounded by the din of war, without being engaged in it.

About a year passed off, and we, as usual, were enjoying ourselves in the employments of peaceable times, when a messenger arrived from the

British Commissioners, requesting all the Indians of our tribe to attend a general council which was soon to be held at Oswego. The council convened, and being opened, the British Commissioners informed the Chiefs that the object of calling a council of the Six Nations, was, to engage their assistance in subduing the rebels, the people of the states, who had risen up against the good King, their master, and were about to rob him of a great part of his possessions and wealth, and added that they would amply reward them for all their services.

The Chiefs then arose, and informed the Commissioners of the nature and extent of the treaty which they had entered into with the people of the states, the year before, and that they should not violate it by taking up the hatchet against them.

The Commissioners continued their entreaties without success, till they addressed their avarice, by telling our people that the people of the states were few in number, and easily subdued; and that on the account of their disobedience to the King, they justly merited all the punishment that it was possible for white men and Indians to inflict upon them; and added, that the King was rich and powerful, both in money and subjects: That his rum was as plenty as the water in lake Ontario: that his men were as numerous as the sands upon the lake shore:—and that the Indians, if they would assist in the war, and persevere in their friendship to the King, till it was closed, should never want for money or goods. Upon this the Chiefs concluded a treaty with the British Commissioners, in which they agreed to take up arms against the rebels, and continue in the service of his Majesty till they were subdued, in consideration of certain conditions which were stipulated in the treaty to be performed by the British government and its agents.

As soon as the treaty was finished, the Commissioners made a present to each Indian of a suit of clothes, a brass kettle, a gun and tomahawk, a scalping knife, a quantity of powder and lead, a piece of gold, and promised a bounty on every scalp that should be brought in. Thus richly clad and equipped, they returned home, after an absence of about two weeks, full of the fire of war, and anxious to encounter their enemies. Many of the kettles which the Indians received at that time are now in use on the Genesee Flats.

Hired to commit depredations upon the whites, who had given them no offence, they waited impatiently to commence their labor, till sometime in the spring of 1776, when a convenient opportunity offered for them to make an attack. At that time, a party of our Indians were at Cau-te-ga, who shot a man that was looking after his horse, for the sole purpose, as I was informed by my Indian brother, who was present, of commencing hostilities.

In May following, our Indians were in their first battle with the Americans; but at what place I am unable to determine. While they were absent at that time, my daughter Nancy was born.

The same year, at Cherry Valley, our Indians took a woman and her three daughters prisoners, and brought them on, leaving one at Canandaigua, one at Honeoy, one at Cattaraugus, and one (the woman) at Little Beard's Town, where I resided. The woman told me that she and her daughters might have escaped, but that they expected the British army only, and therefore made no effort. Her husband and sons got away. Sometime having elapsed, they were redeemed at Fort Niagara by Col. Butler, who clothed them well, and sent them home.

In the same expedition, Joseph Smith was taken prisoner at or near Cherry Valley, brought to Genesee, and detained till after the revolutionary war. He was then liberated, and the Indians made him a present, in company with Horatio Jones, of 6000 acres of land lying in the present town of Leicester, in the county of Livingston.

One of the girls just mentioned, was married to a British officer at Fort Niagara, by the name of Johnson, who at the time she was taken, took a gold ring from her finger, without any compliments or ceremonies. When he saw her at Niagara he recognized her features, restored the ring that he had so impolitely borrowed, and courted and married her.

Previous to the battle at Fort Stanwix, the British sent for the Indians to come and see them whip the rebels; and, at the same time stated that they did not wish to have them fight, but wanted to have them just sit down, smoke their pipes, and look on. Our Indians went, to a man; but contrary to their expectation, instead of smoking and looking on, they were obliged to fight for their lives, and in the end of the battle were completely beaten, with a great loss in killed and wounded. Our Indians alone had thirty-six killed, and a great number wounded. Our town exhibited a scene of real sorrow and distress, when our warriors returned and recounted their misfortunes, and stated the real loss they had sustained in the engagement. The mourning was excessive, and was expressed by the most doleful yells, shrieks, and howlings, and by inimitable gesticulations.

During the revolution, my house was the home of Col's Butler and Brandt, whenever they chanced to come into our neighborhood as they passed to and from Fort Niagara, which was the seat of their military operations. Many and many a night I have pounded samp for them from sun-set till sun-rise, and furnished them with necessary provision and clean clothing for their journey.

✣◉✣◉✣

CHAPTER VII.

Gen. Sullivan with a large army arrives at Canandaigua. Indians' troubles. Determine to stop their march. Skirmish at Connessius Lake. Circumstances attending the Execution of an Oneida warrior. Escape of an Indian Prisoner. Lieut. Boyd and another man taken Prisoners. Cruelty of Boyd's Execution. Indians retreat to the woods. Sullivan comes on to Genesee Flats and destroys the property of the Indians. Returns. Indians return. Mrs. Jemison goes to Gardow. Her Employment there. Attention of an old Negro to her safety, &c. Severe Winter. Sufferings of the Indians. Destruction of Game. Indians' Expedition to the Mohawk Capture old John O'Bail, &c. Other Prisoners taken, &c.

For four or five years we sustained no loss in the war, except in the few who had been killed in distant battles; and our tribe, because of the remoteness of its situation from the enemy, felt secure from an attack. At length, in the fall of 1779, intelligence was received that a large and powerful army of the rebels, under the command of General Sullivan, was making rapid progress towards our settlement, burning and destroying the huts and corn-fields; killing the cattle, hogs and horses, and cutting down the fruit trees belonging to the Indians throughout the country.

Our Indians immediately became alarmed, and suffered every thing but death from fear that they should be taken by surprize, and totally destroyed at a single blow. But in order to prevent so great a catastrophe, they sent out a few spies who were to keep themselves at a short distance in front of the invading army, in order to watch its operations, and give information of its advances and success.

Sullivan arrived at Canandaigua Lake, and had finished his work of destruction there, and it was ascertained that he was about to march to our flats, when our Indians resolved to give him battle on the way, and prevent, if possible, the distresses to which they knew we should be subjected, if he should succeed in reaching our town. Accordingly they sent all their women and children into the woods a little west of Little Beard's Town, in order that we might make a good retreat if it should be necessary, and then, well armed, set out to face the conquering enemy. The place which they fixed upon for their battle ground lay between Honeoy Creek and the head of Connessius Lake.

At length a scouting party from Sullivan's army arrived at the spot selected, when the Indians arose from their ambush with all the fierceness and terror that it was possible for them to exercise, and directly put the party upon a retreat. Two Oneida Indians were all the prisoners that were taken in that skirmish. One of them was a pilot of Gen. Sullivan, and had been very active in the war, rendering to the people of the states essential services. At the commencement of the revolution he had a brother older than himself, who resolved to join the British service, and endeavored by all the art that he was capable of using to persuade his brother to accompany him; but his arguments proved abortive. This went to the British, and that joined the American army. At this critical juncture they met, one in the capacity of a conqueror, the other in that of a prisoner; and as an Indian seldom forgets a countenance that he has seen, they recognized each other at sight. Envy and revenge glared in the features of the conquering savage, as he advanced to his brother (the prisoner) in all the haughtiness of Indian pride, heightened by a sense of power, and addressed him in the following manner:

"Brother, you have merited death! The hatchet or the war-club shall finish your career!—When I begged of you to follow me in the fortunes of war, you was deaf to my cries—you spurned my entreaties!

"Brother! you have merited death and shall

[55]

have your deserts! When the rebels raised their hatchets to fight their good master, you sharpened your knife, you brightened your rifle and led on our foes to the fields of our fathers!—You have merited death and shall die by our hands! When those rebels had drove us from the fields of our fathers to seek out new homes, it was you who could dare to step forth as their pilot, and conduct them even to the doors of our wigwams, to butcher our children and put us to death! No crime can be greater!—But though you have merited death and shall die on this spot, my hands shall not be stained in the blood of a brother! *Who will strike?*"

Little Beard, who was standing by, as soon as the speech was ended, struck the prisoner on the head with his tomahawk, and despatched him at once!

Little Beard then informed the other Indian prisoner that as they were at war with the whites only, and not with the Indians, they would spare his life, and after a while give him his liberty in an honorable manner. The Oneida warrior, however, was jealous of Little Beard's fidelity; and suspecting that he should soon fall by his hands, watched for a favorable opportunity to make his escape; which he soon effected. Two Indians were leading him, one on each side, when he made a violent effort, threw them upon the ground, and run for his life towards where the main body of the American army was encamped. The Indians pursued him without success; but in their absence they fell in with a small detachment of Sullivan's men, with whom they had a short but severe skirmish, in which they killed a number of the enemy, took Capt. or Lieut. William Boyd and one private, prisoners, and brought them to Little Beard's Town, where they were soon after put to death in the most shocking and cruel manner. Little Beard, in this, as in all other scenes of cruelty that happened at his town, was master of ceremonies, and principal actor. Poor Boyd was stripped of his clothing, and then tied to a sapling, where the Indians menaced his life by throwing their tomahawks at the tree, directly over his head, brandishing their scalping knives around him in the most frightful manner, and accompanying their ceremonies with terrific shouts of joy. Having punished him sufficiently in this way, they made a small opening in his abdomen, took out an intestine, which they tied to the sapling, and then unbound him from the tree, and drove him round it till he had drawn out the whole of his intestines. He was then beheaded, his head was stuck upon a pole, and his body left on the ground unburied. Thus ended the life of poor William Boyd, who, it was said, had every appearance of being an active and enterprizing officer, of the first talents. The other prisoner was (if I remember distinctly) only beheaded and left near Boyd.

This tragedy being finished, our Indians again held a short council on the expediency of giving Sullivan battle, if he should continue to advance, and finally came to the conclusion that they were not strong enough to drive him, nor to prevent his taking possession of their fields: but that if it was possible they would escape with their own lives, preserve their families, and leave their possessions to be overrun by the invading army.

The women and children were then sent on still further towards Buffalo, to a large creek that was called by the Indians Catawba, accompanied by a part of the Indians, while the remainder secreted themselves in the woods back of Beard's Town, to watch the movements of the army.

At that time I had three children who went with me on foot, one who rode on horse back, and one whom I carried on my back.

Our corn was good that year; a part of which we had gathered and secured for winter.

In one or two days after the skirmish at Connissius lake, Sullivan and his army arrived at Genesee river, where they destroyed every article of the food kind that they could lay their hands on. A part of our corn they burnt, and threw the remainder into the river. They burnt our houses, killed what few cattle and horses they could find, destroyed our fruit trees, and left nothing but the bare soil and timber. But the Indians had eloped and were not to be found.

Having crossed and recrossed the river, and finished the work of destruction, the army marched off to the east. Our Indians saw them move off, but suspecting that it was Sullivan's intention to watch our return, and then to take us by surprize, resolved that the main body of our tribe should hunt where we then were, till Sullivan had gone so far that there would be no danger of his returning to molest us.

This being agreed to, we hunted continually till

the Indians concluded that there could be no risk in our once more taking possession of our lands. Accordingly we all returned; but what were our feelings when we found that there was not a mouthful of any kind of sustenance left, not even enough to keep a child one day from perishing with hunger.

The weather by this time had become cold and stormy; and as we were destitute of houses and food too, I immediately resolved to take my children and look out for myself, without delay. With this intention I took two of my little ones on my back, bade the other three follow, and the same night arrived on the Gardow flats, where I have ever since resided.

At that time, two negroes, who had run away from their masters sometime before, were the only inhabitants of those flats. They lived in a small cabin and had planted and raised a large field of corn, which they had not yet harvested. As they were in want of help to secure their crop, I hired to them to husk corn till the whole was harvested.

I have laughed a thousand times to myself when I have thought of the good old negro, who hired me, who fearing that I should get taken or injured by the Indians, stood by me constantly when I was husking, with a loaded gun in his hand, in order to keep off the enemy, and thereby lost as much labor of his own as he received from me, by paying good wages. I, however, was not displeased with his attention; for I knew that I should need all the corn that I could earn, even if I should husk the whole. I husked enough for them, to gain for myself, at every tenth string, one hundred strings of ears, which were equal to twenty-five bushels of shelled corn. This seasonable supply made my family comfortable for samp and cakes through the succeeding winter, which was the most severe that I have witnessed since my remembrance. The snow fell about five feet deep, and remained so for a long time, and the weather was extremely cold; so much so indeed, that almost all the game upon which the Indians depended for subsistence, perished, and reduced them almost to a state of starvation through that and three or four succeeding years. When the snow melted in the spring, deer were found dead upon the ground in vast numbers; and other animals, of every description, perished from the cold also, and were found dead, in multitudes. Many of our people barely escaped with their lives, and some actually died of hunger and freezing.

But to return from this digression: Having been completely routed at Little Beard's Town, deprived of a house, and without the means of building one in season, after I had finished my husking, and having found from the short acquaintance which I had had with the negroes, that they were kind and friendly, I concluded, at their request, to take up my residence with them for a while in their cabin, till I should be able to provide a hut for myself. I lived more comfortable than I expected to through the winter, and the next season made a shelter for myself.

The negroes continued on my flats two or three years after this, and then left them for a place that they expected would suit them much better. But as that land became my own in a few years, by virtue of a deed from the Chiefs of the Six Nations, I have lived there from that to the present time.

My flats were cleared before I saw them; and it was the opinion of the oldest Indians that were at Genishau, at the time that I first went there, that all the flats on the Genesee river were improved before any of the Indian tribes ever saw them. I well remember that soon after I went to Little Beard's Town, the banks of Fall-Brook were washed off, which left a large number of human bones uncovered. The Indians then said that those were not the bones of Indians, because they had never heard of any of their dead being buried there; but that they were the bones of a race of men who a great many moons before, cleared that land and lived on the flats.

The next summer after Sullivan's campaign, our Indians, highly incensed at the whites for the treatment they had received, and the sufferings which they had consequently endured, determined to obtain some redress by destroying their frontier settlements. Corn Planter, otherwise called John O'Bail, led the Indians, and an officer by the name of Johnston commanded the British in the expedition. The force was large, and so strongly bent upon revenge and vengeance, that seemingly nothing could avert its march, nor prevent its depredations. After leaving Genesee they marched directly to some of the head waters of the Susquehannah river, and Schoharie Creek, went down that creek to the Mohawk river, thence up that river to Fort Stanwix, and from thence came home. In their route they burnt a number of places; destroyed all the cattle and other property that fell in their way; killed a number of white people, and brought home a few prisoners.

In that expedition, when they came to Fort Plain, on the Mohawk river, Corn Planter and a party of his Indians took old John O'Bail, a white man, and made him a prisoner. Old John O'Bail, in his younger days had frequently passed through the Indian settlements that lay between the Hudson and Fort Niagara, and in some of his excursions had become enamored with a squaw, by whom he had a son that was called Corn Planter.

Corn Planter, was a chief of considerable eminence; and having been informed of his parentage and of the place of his father's residence, took the old man at this time, in order that he might make an introduction leisurely, and become acquainted with a man to whom, though a stranger, he was satisfied that he owed his existence.

After he had taken the old man, his father, he led him as a prisoner ten or twelve miles up the river, and then stepped before him, faced about, and addressed him in the following terms:—

"My name is John O'Bail, commonly called Corn Planter. I am your son! you are my father! You are now my prisoner, and subject to the customs of Indian warfare: but you shall not be harmed; you need not fear. I am a warrior! Many are the scalps which I have taken! Many prisoners I have tortured to death! I am your son! I am a warrior! I was anxious to see you, and to greet you in friendship. I went to your cabin and took you by force! But your life shall be spared. Indians love their friends and their kindred, and treat them with kindness. If now you choose to follow the fortune of your yellow son, and to live with our people, I will cherish your old age with plenty of venison, and you shall live easy: But if it is your choice to return to your fields and live with your white children, I will send a party of my trusty young men to conduct you back in safety. I respect you, my father; you have been friendly to Indians, and they are your friends."

Old John chose to return. Corn Planter, as good as his word, ordered an escort to attend him home, which they did with the greatest care.

Amongst the prisoners that were brought to Genesee, was William Newkirk, a man by the name of Price, and two negroes.

Price lived a while with Little Beard, and afterwards with Jack Berry, an Indian. When he left Jack Berry he went to Niagara, where he now resides.

Newkirk was brought to Beard's Town, and lived with Little Beard and at Fort Niagara about one year, and then enlisted under Butler, and went with him on an expedition to the Monongahela.

❖◉❖◉❖

CHAPTER VIII.

Life of Ebenezer Allen, a Tory. He comes to Gardow. His intimacy with a Nanticoke Squaw. She gives him a Cap. Her Husband's jealousy. Cruelty to his Wife. Hiokatoo's Mandate. Allen supports her. Her Husband is received into favor. Allen labors. Purchases Goods. Stops the Indian War. His troubles with the Indians. Marries a Squaw. Is taken and carried to Quebec. Acquitted. Goes to Philadelphia. Returns to Genesee with

*a Store of Goods, &c. Goes to Farming. Moves to Allen's
Creek. Builds Mills at Rochester. Drowns a Dutchman.
Marries a white Wife. Kills an old Man. Gets a Concubine. Moves to Mt. Morris. Marries a third Wife and
gets another Concubine. Receives a tract of Land. Sends
his Children to other States, &c. Disposes of his Land.
Moves to Grand River, where he dies. His Cruelties.*

SOMETIME near the close of the revolutionary
war, a white man by the name of Ebenezer Allen,
left his people in the state of Pennsylvania on the
account of some disaffection towards his countrymen, and came to the Genesee river, to reside
with the Indians. He tarried at Genishau a few
days, and came up to Gardow, where I then resided.—He was, apparently, without any business
that would support him; but he soon became acquainted with my son Thomas, with whom he
hunted for a long time, and made his home with
him at my house; winter came on, and he continued his stay.

When Allen came to my house, I had a white
man living on my land, who had a Nanticoke
squaw for his wife, with whom he had lived very
peaceably; for he was a moderate man commonly,
and she was a kind, gentle, cunning creature. It
so happened that he had no hay for his cattle; so
that in the winter he was obliged to drive them
every day, perhaps half a mile from his house, to
let them feed on rushes, which in those days were
so numerous as to nearly cover the ground.

Allen having frequently seen the squaw in the
fall, took the opportunity when her husband was
absent with his cows, daily to make her a visit;

and in return for his kindness she made and gave him a red cap finished and decorated in the highest Indian style.

The husband had for some considerable length of time felt a degree of jealousy that Allen was trespassing upon him with the consent of his squaw; but when he saw Allen dressed in so fine an Indian cap, and found that his dear Nanticoke had presented it to him, his doubts all left him, and he became so violently enraged that he caught her by the hair of her head, dragged her on the ground to my house, a distance of forty rods, and threw her in at the door. Hiokatoo, my husband, exasperated at the sight of so much inhumanity, hastily took down his old tomahawk, which for awhile had lain idle, shook it over the cuckold's head, and bade him jogo (i. e. go off.) The enraged husband, well knowing that he should feel a blow if he waited to hear the order repeated, instantly retreated, and went down the river to his cattle. We protected the poor Nanticoke woman, and gave her victuals; and Allen sympathized with her in her misfortunes till spring, when her husband came to her, acknowledged his former errors, and that he had abused her without a cause, promised a reformation, and she received him with every mark of a renewal of her affection. They went home lovingly, and soon after removed to Niagara.

The same spring, Allen commenced working my flats, and continued to labor there till after the peace in 1783. He then went to Philadelphia on some business that detained him but a few days, and returned with a horse and some dry goods, which he carried to a place that is now called Mount Morris, where he built or bought a small house.

The British and Indians on the Niagara frontier, dissatisfied with the treaty of peace, were determined, at all hazards, to continue their depredations upon the white settlements which lay between them and Albany. They actually made ready, and were about setting out on an expedition to that effect, when Allen (who by this time understood their customs of war) took a belt of wampum, which he had fraudulently procured, and carried it as a token of peace from the Indians to the commander of the nearest American military post.

The Indians were soon answered by the American officer that the wampum was cordially accepted; and, that a continuance of peace was ardently wished for. The Indians, at this, were chagrined and disappointed beyond measure; but as they held the wampum to be a sacred thing, they dared not to go against the import of its meaning, and immediately buried the hatchet as it respected the people of the United States; and smoked the pipe of peace. They, however, resolved to punish Allen for his officiousness in meddling with their national affairs, by presenting the sacred wampum without their knowledge, and went about devising means for his detection. A party was accordingly despatched from Fort Niagara to apprehend him; with orders to conduct him to that post for trial, or for safe keeping, till such time as his fate should be determined upon in a legal manner.

The party came on; but before it arrived at

Gardow, Allen got news of its approach, and fled for safety, leaving the horse and goods that he had brought from Philadelphia, an easy prey to his enemies. He had not been long absent when they arrived at Gardow, where they made diligent search for him till they were satisfied that they could not find him, and then seized the effects which he had left, and returned to Niagara. My son Thomas, went with them, with Allen's horse, and carried the goods.

Allen, on finding that his enemies had gone, came back to my house, where he lived as before; but of his return they were soon notified at Niagara, and Nettles (who married Priscilla Ramsay) with a small party of Indians came on to take him. He, however, by some means found that they were near, and gave me his box of money and trinkets to keep safely, till he called for it, and again took to the woods.

Nettles came on determined at all events to take him before he went back; and, in order to accomplish his design, he, with his Indians, hunted in the day time and lay by at night at my house, and in that way they practised for a number of days. Allen watched the motion of his pursuers, and every night after they had gone to rest, came home and got some food, and then returned to his retreat. It was in the fall, and the weather was cold and rainy, so that he suffered extremely. Some nights he sat in my chamber till nearly daybreak, while his enemies were below, and when the time arrived I assisted him to escape unnoticed.

Nettles at length abandoned the chase—went

home, and Allen, all in tatters, came in. By running in the woods his clothing had become torn into rags, so that he was in a suffering condition, almost naked. Hiokatoo gave him a blanket, and a piece of broadcloth for a pair of trowsers. Allen made his trowsers himself, and then built a raft, on which he went down the river to his own place at Mount Morris.

About that time he married a squaw, whose name was Sally.

The Niagara people finding that he was at his own house, came and took him by surprize when he least expected them, and carried him to Niagara. Fortunately for him, it so happened that just as they arrived at the fort, a house took fire and his keepers all left him to save the building, if possible. Allen had supposed his doom to be nearly sealed; but finding himself at liberty he took to his heels, left his escort to put out the fire, and ran to Tonnawanta. There an Indian give him some refreshment, and a good gun, with which he hastened on to Little Beard's Town, where he found his squaw. Not daring to risk himself at that place for fear of being given up, he made her but a short visit, and came immediately to Gardow.

Just as he got to the top of the hill above the Gardow flats, he discovered a party of British soldiers and Indians in pursuit of him; and in fact they were so near that he was satisfied that they saw him, and concluded that it would be impossible for him to escape. The love of liberty, however, added to his natural swiftness, gave him sufficient strength to make his escape to his former castle of safety. His pursuers came immediately to my house, where they expected to have found him secreted, and under my protection. They told me where they had seen him but a few moments before, and that they were confident that it was within my power to put him into their hands. As I was perfectly clear of having had any hand in his escape, I told them plainly that I had not seen him since he was taken to Niagara, and that I could give them no information at all respecting him. Still unsatisfied, and doubting my veracity, they advised my Indian brother to use his influence to draw from me the secret of his concealment, which they had an idea that I considered of great importance, not only to him but to myself. I persisted in my ignorance of his situation, and finally they left me.

Although I had not seen Allen, I knew his place of security, and was well aware that if I told them the place where he had formerly hid himself, they would have no difficulty in making him a prisoner.

He came to my house in the night, and awoke me with the greatest caution, fearing that some of his enemies might be watching to take him at a time when, and in a place where it would be impossible for him to make his escape. I got up and assured him that he was then safe; but that his enemies would return early in the morning and search him out if it should be possible. Having given him some victuals, which he received thankfully, I told him to go, but to return the next night to a certain corner of the fence near my house where he would find a quantity of meal that I would have well prepared and deposited there for his use.

Early the next morning, Nettles and his company came in while I was pounding the meal for Allen, and insisted upon my giving him up. I again told them that I did not know where he was, and that I could not, neither would I, tell them any thing about him. I well knew that Allen considered his life in my hands; and although it was my intention not to lie, I was fully determined to keep his situation a profound secret. They continued their labor and examined (as they supposed) every crevice, gully, tree and hollow log in the neighboring woods, and at last concluded that he had left the country, and gave him up for lost, and went home.

At that time Allen lay in a secret place in the gulph a short distance above my flats, in a hole that he accidentally found in the rock near the river. At night he came and got the meal at the corner of the fence as I had directed him, and afterwards lived in the gulph two weeks. Each night he came to the pasture and milked one of my cows, without any other vessel in which to receive the milk than his hat, out of which he drank it. I supplied him with meal, but fearing to build a fire he was obliged to eat it raw and wash it down with the milk. Nettles having left our neighborhood, and Allen considering himself safe, left his little cave and came home. I gave him his box of money and trinkets, and he went to his own house at Mount Morris. It was generally considered by the Indians of our tribe, that Allen was an innocent

man, and that the Niagara people were persecut-
ing him without a just cause. Little Beard, then
about to go to the eastward on public business,
charged his Indians not to meddle with Allen, but
to let him live amongst them peaceably, and enjoy
himself with his family and property if he could.
Having the protection of the chief, he felt himself
safe, and let his situation be known to the whites
from whom he suspected no harm. They, however,
were more inimical than our Indians and were easily bribed by Nettles to assist in bringing him to
justice. Nettles came on, and the whites, as they
had agreed, gave poor Allen up to him. He was
bound and carried to Niagara, where he was confined in prison through the winter. In the spring
he was taken to Montreal or Quebec for trial, and
was honorably acquitted. The crime for which he
was tried was, for his having carried the wampum
to the Americans, and thereby putting too sudden
a stop to their war.

From the place of his trial he went directly to
Philadelphia, and purchased on credit, a boat load
of goods which he brought by water to Conhocton,
where he left them and came to Mount Morris for
assistance to get them brought on. The Indians
readily went with horses and brought them to his
house, where he disposed of his dry goods; but not
daring to let the Indians begin to drink strong
liquor, for fear of the quarrels which would naturally follow, he sent his spirits to my place and
we sold them. For his goods he received ginseng
roots, principally, and a few skins. Ginseng at that
time was plenty, and commanded a high price. We

prepared the whole that he received for the market, expecting that he would carry them to Philadelphia. In that I was disappointed; for when he had disposed of, and got pay for all his goods, he took the ginseng and skins to Niagara, and there sold them and came home.

Tired of dealing in goods, he planted a large field of corn on or near his own land, attended to it faithfully, and succeeded in raising a large crop, which he harvested, loaded into canoes and carried down the river to the mouth of Allen's Creek, then called by the Indian Gin-is-a-ga, where he unloaded it, built him a house, and lived with his family.

The next season he planted corn at that place and built a grist and saw mill on Genesee Falls, now called Rochester.

At the time Allen built the mills, he had an old German living with him by the name of Andrews, whom he sent in a canoe down the river with his mill irons. Allen went down at the same time; but before they got to the mills Allen threw the old man overboard and drowned him, as it was then generally believed, for he was never seen or heard of afterwards.

In the course of the season in which Allen built his mills, he became acquainted with the daughter of a white man, who was moving to Niagara. She was handsome, and Allen soon got into her good graces, so that he married and took her home, to be a joint partner with Sally, the squaw, whom she had never heard of till she got home and found her in full possession; but it was too late for her to retrace the hasty steps she had taken, for her father had left her in the care of a tender husband and gone on. She, however, found that she enjoyed at least an equal half of her husband's affections, and made herself contented. Her father's name I have forgotten, but her's was Lucy.

Allen was not contented with two wives, for in a short time after he had married Lucy he came up to my house, where he found a young woman who had an old husband with her. They had been on a long journey, and called at my place to recruit and rest themselves. She filled Allen's eye, and he accordingly fixed upon a plan to get her into his possession. He praised his situation, enumerated his advantages, and finally persuaded them to go home and tarry with him a few days at least, and partake of a part of his comforts. They accepted his generous invitation and went home with him. But they had been there but two or three days when Allen took the old gentleman out to view his flats; and as they were deliberately walking on the bank of the river, pushed him into the water. The old man, almost strangled, succeeded in getting out; but his fall and exertions had so powerful an effect upon his system that he died in two or three days, and left his young widow to the protection of his murderer. She lived with him about one year in a state of concubinage and then left him.

How long Allen lived at Allen's Creek I am unable to state; but soon after the young widow left him, he removed to his old place at Mount Morris, and built a house, where he made Sally, his squaw, by whom he had two daughters, a slave to Lucy, by whom he had had one son; still, however, he considered Sally to be his wife.

After Allen came to Mt. Morris at that time, he married a girl by the name of Morilla Gregory, whose father at the time lived on Genesee Flats. The ceremony being over, he took her home to live in common with his other wives; but his house was too small for his family; for Sally and Lucy, conceiving that their lawful privileges would be abridged if they received a partner, united their strength and whipped poor Morilla so cruelly that he was obliged to keep her in a small Indian house a short distance from his own, or lose her entirely. Morilla, before she left Mt. Morris, had four children.

One of Morilla's sisters lived with Allen about a year after Morilla was married, and then quit him.

A short time after they all got to living at Mt. Morris, Allen prevailed upon the Chiefs to give to his Indian children, a tract of land four miles square, where he then resided. The Chiefs gave them the land, but he so artfully contrived the conveyance, that he could apply it to his own use, and by alienating his right, destroy the claim of his children.

Having secured the land, in that way, to himself, he sent his two Indian girls to Trenton, (N. J.) and his white son to Philadelphia, for the purpose of giving each of them a respectable English education.

While his children were at school, he went to Philadelphia, and sold his right to the land which he had begged of the Indians for his children to Robert Morris. After that, he sent for his daughters to come home, which they did.

Having disposed of the whole of his property

on the Genesee river, he took his two white wives and their children, together with his effects, and removed to a Delaware town on the river De Trench, in Upper Canada. When he left Mt. Morris, Sally, his squaw, insisted upon going with him, and actually followed him, crying bitterly, and praying for his protection some two or three miles, till he absolutely bade her leave him, or he would punish her with severity.

At length, finding her case hopeless, she returned to the Indians.

At the great treaty at Big Tree, one of Allen's daughters claimed the land which he had sold to Morris. The claim was examined and decided against her in favor of Ogden, Trumbull, Rogers and others, who were the creditors of Robert Morris. Allen yet believed that his daughter had an indisputable right to the land in question, and got me to go with mother Farly, a half Indian woman, to assist him by interceding with Morris for it, and to urge the propriety of her claim. We went to Thomas Morris, and having stated to him our business, he told us plainly that he had no land to give away, and that as the title was good, he never would allow Allen, nor his heirs, one foot, or words to that effect. We returned to Allen the answer we had received, and he, conceiving all further attempts to be useless, went home.

He died at the Delaware town, on the river De Trench, in the year 1814 or 15, and left two white widows and one squaw, with a number of children, to lament his loss.

By his last will he gave all his property to his

last wife, (Morilla,) and her children, without providing in the least for the support of Lucy, or any of the other members of his family. Lucy, soon after his death, went with her children down the Ohio river, to receive assistance from her friends.

In the revolutionary war, Allen was a tory, and by that means became acquainted with our Indians, when they were in the neighborhood of his native place, desolating the settlements on the Susquehannah. In those predatory battles, he joined them, and (as I have often heard the Indians say,) for cruelty was not exceeded by any of his Indian comrades!

At one time, when he was scouting with the Indians in the Susquehannah country, he entered a house very early in the morning, where he found a man, his wife, and one child, in bed. The man, as he entered the door, instantly sprang on the floor, for the purpose of defending himself and little family; but Allen dispatched him at one blow. He then cut off his head and threw it bleeding into the bed with the terrified woman; took the little infant from its mother's breast, and holding it by its legs, dashed its head against the jamb, and left the unhappy widow and mother to mourn alone over her murdered family. It has been said by some, that after he had killed the child, he opened the fire and buried it under the coals and embers: But of that I am not certain. I have often heard him speak of that transaction with a great degree of sorrow, and as the foulest crime he had ever committed—one for which I have no doubt he repented.

CHAPTER IX.

Mrs. Jemison has liberty to go to her Friends. Chooses to stay. Her Reasons, &c. Her Indian Brother makes provisions for her Settlement. He goes to Grand River and dies. Her Love for him, &c. She is presented with the Gardow Reservation. Is troubled by Speculators. Description of the Soil, &c. of her Flats. Indian notions of the ancient Inhabitants of this Country.

Soon after the close of the revolutionary war, my Indian brother, Kau-jises-tau-ge-au (which being interpreted signifies Black Coals,) offered me my liberty, and told me that if it was my choice I might go to my friends.

My son, Thomas, was anxious that I should go; and offered to go with me and assist me on the journey, by taking care of the younger children, and providing food as we travelled through the wilderness. But the Chiefs of our tribe, suspecting from his appearance, actions, and a few warlike exploits, that Thomas would be a great warrior, or a good counsellor, refused to let him leave them on any account whatever.

To go myself, and leave him, was more than I felt able to do; for he had been kind to me, and was one on whom I placed great dependence. The Chiefs refusing to let him go, was one reason for my resolving to stay; but another, more powerful, if possible, was, that I had got a large family of Indian children, that I must take with me; and that if I should be so fortunate as to find my relatives, they would despise them, if not myself;

and treat us as enemies; or, at least with a degree of cold indifference, which I thought I could not endure.

Accordingly, after I had duly considered the matter, I told my brother that it was my choice to stay and spend the remainder of my days with my Indian friends, and live with my family as I had heretofore done. He appeared well pleased with my resolution, and informed me, that as that was my choice, I should have a piece of land that I could call my own, where I could live unmolested, and have something at my decease to leave for the benefit of my children.

In a short time he made himself ready to go to Upper Canada; but before he left us, he told me that he would speak to some of the Chiefs at Buffalo, to attend the great Council, which he expected would convene in a few years at farthest, and convey to me such a tract of land as I should select. My brother left us, as he had proposed, and soon after died at Grand River.

Kaujisestaugeau, was an excellent man, and ever treated me with kindness. Perhaps no one of his tribe at any time exceeded him in natural mildness of temper, and warmth and tenderness of affection. If he had taken my life at the time when the avarice of the old King inclined him to procure my emancipation, it would have been done with a pure heart and from good motives. He loved his friends; and was generally beloved. During the time that I lived in the family with him, he never offered the most trifling abuse; on the contrary, his whole conduct towards me was strictly honorable. I mourned his loss as that of a tender brother, and shall recollect him through life with emotions of friendship and gratitude.

I lived undisturbed, without hearing a word on the subject of my land, till the great Council was held at Big Tree, in 1797, when Farmer's Brother, whose Indian name is Ho-na-ye-wus, sent for me to attend the council. When I got there, he told me that my brother had spoken to him to see that I had a piece of land reserved for my use; and that then was the time for me to receive it.—He requested that I would choose for myself and describe the bounds of a piece that would suit me. I accordingly told him the place of beginning, and then went round a tract that I judged would be sufficient for my purpose, (knowing that it would include the Gardow Flats,) by stating certain bounds with which I was acquainted.

When the Council was opened, and the business afforded a proper opportunity, Farmer's Brother presented my claim, and rehearsed the request of my brother. Red Jacket, whose Indian name is Sagu-yu-what-hah, which interpreted, is Keeper-awake, opposed me or my claim with all his influence and eloquence. Farmer's Brother insisted upon the necessity, propriety and expediency of his proposition, and got the land granted. The deed was made and signed, securing to me the title to all the land I had described; under the same restrictions and regulations that other Indian lands are subject to.

That land has ever since been known by the name of the Gardow Tract.

Red Jacket not only opposed my claim at the Council, but he withheld my money two or three years, on the account of my lands having been granted without his consent. Parrish and Jones at length convinced him that it was the white people, and not the Indians who had given me the land, and compelled him to pay over all the money which he had retained on my account.

My land derived its name, Gardow, from a hill that is within its limits, which is called in the Seneca language Kau-tam. Kautam when interpreted signifies up and down, or down and up, and is applied to a hill that you will ascend and descend in passing it; or to a valley. It has been said that Gardow was the name of my husband Hiokatoo, and that my land derived its name from him; that however was a mistake, for the old man always considered Gardow a nickname, and was uniformly offended when called by it.

About three hundred acres of my land, when I first saw it, was open flats, lying on the Genesee River, which it is supposed was cleared by a race of inhabitants who preceded the first Indian settlements in this part of the country. The Indians are confident that many parts of this country were settled and for a number of years occupied by people of whom their fathers never had any tradition, as they never had seen them. Whence those people originated, and whither they went, I have never heard one of our oldest and wisest Indians pretend to guess. When I first came to Genishau, the bank of Fall Brook had just slid off and exposed a large number of human bones, which the

Indians said were buried there long before their fathers ever saw the place; and that they did not know what kind of people they were. It however was and is believed by our people, that they were not Indians.

My flats were extremely fertile; but needed more labor than my daughters and myself were able to perform, to produce a sufficient quantity of grain and other necessary productions of the earth, for the consumption of our family. The land had lain uncultivated so long that it was thickly covered with weeds of almost every description. In order that we might live more easy, Mr. Parrish, with the consent of the chiefs, gave me liberty to lease or let my land to white people to till on shares. I accordingly let it out, and have continued to do so, which makes my task less burthensome, while at the same time I am more comfortably supplied with the means of support.

❖◎❖◎❖

CHAPTER X.

Happy situation of her Family. Disagreement between her sons Thomas and John. Her Advice to them, &c. John kills Thomas. Her Affliction. Council. Decision of the Chiefs, &c. Life of Thomas. His Wives, Children, &c. Cause of his Death, &c.

I HAVE frequently heard it asserted by white people, and can truly say from my own experience, that the time at which parents take the most satisfaction and comfort with their families is when their children are young, incapable of providing for their own wants, and are about the fireside, where they can be daily observed and instructed.

Few mothers, perhaps, have had less trouble with their children during their minority than myself. In general, my children were friendly to each other, and it was very seldom that I knew them to have the least difference or quarrel: so far, indeed, were they from rendering themselves or me uncomfortable, that I considered myself happy—more so than commonly falls to the lot of parents, especially to women.

My happiness in this respect, however, was not without alloy; for my son Thomas, from some cause unknown to me, from the time he was a small lad, always called his brother John, a witch, which was the cause, as they grew towards manhood, of frequent and severe quarrels between them, and gave me much trouble and anxiety for their safety. After Thomas and John arrived to manhood, in addition to the former charge, John got two wives, with whom he lived till the time of his death. Although polygamy was tolerated in our tribe, Thomas considered it a violation of good and wholesome rules in society, and tending directly to destroy that friendly social intercourse and love, that ought to be the happy result of matrimony and chastity. Consequently, he frequently reprimanded John, by telling him that his conduct was beneath the dignity, and inconsistent with the principles of good Indians; indecent and unbecoming a gentleman; and, as he never could reconcile himself to it, he was frequently, almost constantly, when they were together, talking to him on the same subject. John always resented such reprimand, and reproof, with a great degree of passion, though they never quarrelled, unless Thomas was intoxicated.

In his fits of drunkenness, Thomas seemed to lose all his natural reason, and to conduct like a wild or crazy man, without regard to relatives, decency or propriety. At such times he often threatened to take my life for having raised a witch, (as he called John,) and has gone so far as to raise his tomahawk to split my head. He, however, never struck me; but on John's account he struck Hiokatoo, and thereby excited in John a high degree of indignation, which was extinguished only by blood.

For a number of years their difficulties, and consequent unhappiness, continued and rather increased, continually exciting in my breast the most fearful apprehensions, and greatest anxiety for their safety. With tears in my eyes, I advised them to become reconciled to each other, and to be friendly; told them the consequences of their continuing to cherish so much malignity and malice, that it would end in their destruction, the disgrace of their families, and bring me down to the grave. No one can conceive of the constant trouble that I daily endured on their account—on the account of my two oldest sons, whom I loved equally, and with all the feelings and affection of a tender mother, stimulated by an anxious concern for their fate. Parents, mothers especially, will love their children, though ever so unkind and disobedient.

Their eyes of compassion, of real sentimental affection, will be involuntarily extended after them, in their greatest excesses of iniquity; and those fine filaments of consanguinity, which gently entwine themselves around the heart where filial love and parental care is equal, will be lengthened, and enlarged to cords seemingly of sufficient strength to reach and reclaim the wanderer. I know that such exercises are frequently unavailing; but, notwithstanding their ultimate failure, it still remains true, and ever will, that the love of a parent for a disobedient child, will increase, and grow more and more ardent, so long as a hope of its reformation is capable of stimulating a disappointed breast.

My advice and expostulations with my sons were abortive; and year after year their disaffection for each other increased. At length, Thomas came to my house on the 1st day of July, 1811, in my absence, somewhat intoxicated, where he found John, with whom he immediately commenced a quarrel on their old subjects of difference.— John's anger became desperate. He caught Thomas by the hair of his head, dragged him out at the door and there killed him, by a blow which he gave him on the head with his tomahawk!

I returned soon after, and found my son lifeless at the door, on the spot where he was killed! No one can judge of my feelings on seeing this mournful spectacle; and what greatly added to my distress, was the fact that he had fallen by the murderous hand of his brother! I felt my situation unsupportable. Having passed through various scenes of trouble of the most cruel and trying kind, I had hoped to spend my few remaining days in quietude, and to die in peace, surrounded by my family. This fatal event, however, seemed to be a stream of woe poured into my cup of afflictions, filling it even to overflowing, and blasting all my prospects.

As soon as I had recovered a little from the shock which I felt at the sight of my departed son, and some of my neighbors had come in to assist in taking care of the corpse, I hired Shanks, an Indian, to go to Buffalo, and carry the sorrowful news of Thomas' death, to our friends at that place, and request the Chiefs to hold a Council, and dispose of John as they should think proper. Shanks set out on his errand immediately, and John, fearing that he should be apprehended and punished for the crime he had committed, at the same time went off towards Caneadea.

Thomas was decently interred in a style corresponding with his rank.

The Chiefs soon assembled in council on the trial of John, and after having seriously examined the matter according to their laws, justified his conduct, and acquitted him. They considered Thomas to have been the first transgressor, and that for the abuses which he had offered, he had merited from John the treatment that he had received.

John, on learning the decision of the council, returned to his family.

Thomas (except when intoxicated, which was not frequent,) was a kind and tender child, willing to assist me in my labor, and to remove every obstacle to my comfort. His natural abilities were said to be of a superior cast, and he soared above the trifling subjects of revenge, which are common amongst Indians, as being far beneath his attention. In his childish and boyish days, his natural turn was to practise in the art of war, though he despised the cruelties that the warriors inflicted upon their subjugated enemies. He was manly in his deportment, courageous and active; and commanded respect. Though he appeared well pleased with peace, he was cunning in Indian warfare, and succeeded to admiration in the execution of his plans.

At the age of fourteen or fifteen years, he went into the war with manly fortitude, armed with a tomahawk and scalping knife; and when he returned, brought one white man a prisoner, whom he had taken with his own hands, on the west branch of the Susquehannah river. It so happened, that as he was looking out for his enemies, he discovered two men boiling sap in the woods. He watched them unperceived, till dark when he advanced with a noiseless step to where they were standing, caught one of them before they were apprized of danger, and conducted him to the camp. He was well treated while a prisoner, and redeemed at the close of the war.

At the time Kaujisestaugeau gave me my liberty to go to my friends, Thomas was anxious to go with me; but as I have before observed, the Chiefs would not suffer him to leave them on the account of his courage and skill in war: expecting that they should need his assistance. He was a great Counsellor and a Chief when quite young; and in the last capacity, went two or three times to Philadelphia to assist in making treaties with the people of the states.

Thomas had four wives, by whom he had eight children. Jacob Jemison, his second son by his last wife, who is at this time twenty-seven or twenty-eight years of age, went to Dartmouth college, in the spring of 1816, for the purpose of receiving a good education, where it was said that he was an industrious scholar, and made great proficiency in the study of the different branches to which he attended. Having spent two years at that Institution, he returned in the winter of 1818, and is now at Buffalo; where I have understood that he contemplates commencing the study of medicine, as a profession.

Thomas, at the time he was killed, was a few moons over fifty-two years old, and John was forty-eight. As he was naturally good natured, and possessed a friendly disposition, he would not have come to so untimely an end, had it not been for his intemperance. He fell a victim to the use of ardent spirits—a poison that will soon exterminate the Indian tribes in this part of the country, and leave their names without a root or branch. The thought is melancholy; but no arguments, no examples, however persuasive or impressive, are sufficient to deter an Indian for an hour from taking the potent draught, which he knows at the time will derange his faculties, reduce him to a level with the beasts, or deprive him of life!

THE LIFE OF

CHAPTER XI.

*Death of Hiokatoo. Biography. His Birth. Education-
Goes against the Cherokees, &c. Bloody Battles, &c
His success and cruelties in the French War. Battle at
Fort Freeland. Capts. Dougherty and Boon killed. His
Cruelties in the neighborhood of Cherry Valley, &c. In-
dians remove their general Encampment. In 1782, Col.
Crawford is sent to destroy them, &c. Is met by a Traitor.
Battle. Crawford's Men surprized. Irregular Retreat.
Crawford and Doct. Night taken. Council. Crawford
Condemned and Burnt. Aggravating Circumstances.
Night is sentenced to be Burnt. Is Painted by Hiokatoo.
Is conducted off, &c. His fortunate Escape. Hiokatoo
in the French War takes Col. Canton. His Sentence. Is
bound on a wild Colt that runs loose three days. Returns
Alive. Is made to run the Gauntlet. Gets knocked down,
&c. Is Redeemed and sent Home. Hiokatoo's Enmity to
the Cherokees, &c. His Height—Strength—Speed, &c.*

IN the month of November 1811, my husband
Hiokatoo, who had been sick four years of the consumption, died at the advanced age of one hundred
and three years, as nearly as the time could be
estimated. He was the last that remained to me
of our family connection, or rather of my old
friends with whom I was adopted, except a part of
one family, which now lives at Tonewanta.

Hiokatoo was buried decently, and had all the
insignia of a veteran warrior buried with him;
consisting of a war club, tomahawk and scalping
knife, a powder-flask, flint, a piece of spunk, a
small cake and a cup; and in his best clothing.

Hiokatoo was an old man when I first saw him;
but he was by no means enervated. During the

term of nearly fifty years that I lived with him, I received, according to Indian customs, all the kindness and attention that was my due as his wife.—Although war was his trade from his youth till old age and decrepitude stopt his career, he uniformly treated me with tenderness, and never offered an insult.

I have frequently heard him repeat the history of his life from his childhood; and when he came to that part which related to his actions, his bravery and his valor in war; when he spoke of the ambush, the combat, the spoiling of his enemies and the sacrifice of the victims, his nerves seemed strung with youthful ardor, the warmth of the able warrior seemed to animate his frame, and to produce the heated gestures which he had practised in middle age. He was a man of tender feelings to his friends, ready and willing to assist them in distress, yet, as a warrior, his cruelties to his enemies perhaps were unparalleled, and will not admit a word of palliation.

Hiokatoo, was born in one of the tribes of the Six Nations that inhabited the banks of the Susquehannah; or, rather he belonged to a tribe of the Senecas that made, at the time of the great Indian treaty, a part of those nations. He was own cousin to Farmer's Brother, a Chief who has been justly celebrated for his worth. Their mothers were sisters, and it was through the influence of Farmer's Brother, that I became Hiokatoo's wife.

In early life, Hiokatoo showed signs of thirst for blood, by attending only to the art of war, in the use of the tomahawk and scalping knife; and in practising cruelties upon every thing that chanced to fall into his hands, which was susceptible of pain. In that way he learned to use his implements of war effectually, and at the same time blunted all those fine feelings and tender sympathies that are naturally excited, by hearing or seeing, a fellow being in distress. He could inflict the most excruciating tortures upon his enemies, and prided himself upon his fortitude, in having performed the most barbarous ceremonies and tortures, without the least degree of pity or remorse. Thus qualified, when very young he was initiated into scenes of carnage, by being engaged in the wars that prevailed amongst the Indian tribes.

In the year 1731, he was appointed a runner, to assist in collecting an army to go against the Cotawpes, Cherokees and other southern Indians. A large army was collected, and after a long and fatiguing march, met its enemies in what was then called the "low, dark and bloody lands," near the mouth of Red River, in what is now called the state of Kentucky.* The Cotawpes† and their associates, had, by some means, been apprized of their approach, and lay in ambush to take them at once, when they should come within their reach,

*Those powerful armies met near the place that is now called Clarksville, which is situated at the fork where Red River joins the Cumberland, a few miles above the line between Kentucky and Tennessee.

†The Author acknowledges himself unacquainted, from Indian history, with a nation of this name; but as 90 years have elapsed since the date of this occurrence, it is highly probable that such a nation did exist, and that it was absolutely exterminated at that eventful period.

and destroy the whole army. The northern Indians, with their usual sagacity, discovered the situation of their enemies, rushed upon the ambuscade and massacred 1200 on the spot. The battle continued for two days and two nights, with the utmost severity, in which the northern Indians were victorious, and so far succeeded in destroying the Cotawpes that they at that time ceased to be a nation. The victors suffered an immense loss in killed; but gained the hunting ground, which was their grand object, though the Cherokees would not give it up in a treaty, or consent to make peace. Bows and arrows, at that time, were in general use, though a few guns were employed.

From that time he was engaged in a number of battles in which Indians only were engaged, and made fighting his business, till the commencement of the French war. In those battles he took a number of Indians prisoners, whom he killed by tying them to trees and then setting small Indian boys to shooting at them with arrows, till death finished the misery of the sufferers; a process that frequently took two days for its completion!

During the French war he was in every battle that was fought on the Susquehannah and Ohio rivers; and was so fortunate as never to have been taken prisoner.

At Braddock's defeat he took two white prisoners, and burnt them alive in a fire of his own kindling.

In 1777, he was in the battle at Fort Freeland, in Northumberland county, Penn. The fort contained a great number of women and children, and was defended only by a small garrison. The force that went against it consisted of 100 British regulars, commanded by a Col. McDonald, and 300 Indians under Hiokatoo. After a short but bloody engagement, the fort was surrendered; the women and children were sent under an escort to the next fort below, and the men and boys taken off by a party of British to the general Indian encampment. As soon as the fort had capitulated and the firing had ceased, Hiokatoo with the help of a few Indians tomahawked every wounded American while earnestly begging with uplifted hands for quarters.

The massacre was but just finished when Capts. Dougherty and Boon arrived with a reinforcement to assist the garrison. On their arriving in sight of the fort they saw that it had surrendered, and that an Indian was holding the flag. This so much inflamed Capt. Dougherty that he left his command, stept forward and shot the Indian at the first fire. Another took the flag, and had no sooner got it erected than Dougherty dropt him as he had the first. A third presumed to hold it, who was also shot down by Dougherty. Hiokatoo, exasperated at the sight of such bravery, sallied out with a party of his Indians, and killed Capts. Dougherty, Boon, and fourteen men, at the first fire. The remainder of the two companies escaped by taking to flight, and soon arrived at the fort which they had left but a few hours before.

In an expedition that went out against Cherry Valley and the neighboring settlements, Captain David, a Mohawk Indian, was first, and Hiokatoo the second in command. The force consisted of several hundred Indians, who were determined on mischief, and the destruction of the whites. A continued series of wantonness and barbarity characterized their career, for they plundered and burnt every thing that came in their way, and killed a number of persons, among whom were several infants, whom Hiokatoo butchered or dashed upon the stones with his own hands. Besides the instances which have been mentioned, he was in a number of parties during the revolutionary war, where he ever acted a conspicuous part.

The Indians having removed the seat of their depredations and war to the frontiers of Pennsylvania, Ohio, Kentucky and the neighboring territories, assembled a large force at Upper Sandusky, their place of general rendezvous, from whence they went out to the various places which they designed to sacrifice.

Tired of the desolating scenes that were so often witnessed, and feeling a confidence that the savages might be subdued, and an end put to their crimes, the American government raised a regiment, consisting of 300 volunteers, for the purpose of dislodging them from their cantonment and preventing further barbarities. Col. William Crawford and Lieut. Col. David Williamson, men who had been thoroughly tried and approved, were commissioned by Gen. Washington to take the command of a service that seemed all-important to the welfare of the country. In the month of July, 1782, well armed and provided with a sufficient quantity of provision, this regiment made an expeditious march through the wilderness to

Upper Sandusky, where, as had been anticipated, they found the Indians assembled in full force at their encampment, prepared to receive an attack.

As Col. Crawford and his brave band advanced, and when they had got within a short distance from the town, they were met by a white man, with a flag of truce from the Indians, who proposed to Col. Crawford that if he would surrender himself and his men to the Indians, their lives should be spared; but, that if they persisted in their undertaking, and attacked the town, they should all be massacred to a man.

Crawford, while hearing the proposition, attentively surveyed its bearer, and recognized in his features one of his former schoolmates and companions, with whom he was perfectly acquainted, by the name of Simon Gurty. Gurty, but a short time before this, had been a soldier in the American army, in the same regiment with Crawford; but on the account of his not having received the promotion that he expected, he became disaffected —swore an eternal war with his countrymen, fled to the Indians, and joined them, as a leader well qualified to conduct them to where they could satiate their thirst for blood, upon the innocent, unoffending and defenceless settlers.

Crawford sternly inquired of the traitor if his name was not Simon Gurty; and being answered in the affirmative, he informed him that he despised the offer which he had made; and that he should not surrender his army unless he should be compelled to do so, by a superior force.

Gurty returned, and Crawford immediately commenced an engagement that lasted till night, without the appearance of victory on either side, when the firing ceased, and the combatants on both sides retired to take refreshment, and to rest through the night. Crawford encamped in the woods near half a mile from the town, where, after the centinels were placed, and each had taken his ration, they slept on their arms, that they might be instantly ready in case they should be attacked. The stillness of death hovered over the little army, and sleep relieved the whole, except the wakeful centinels who vigilantly attended to their duty.— But what was their surprise, when they found late in the night, that they were surrounded by the Indians on every side, except a narrow space between them and the town? Every man was under arms, and the officers instantly consulted each other on the best method of escaping; for they saw that to fight, would be useless, and that to surrender, would be death.

Crawford proposed to retreat through the ranks of the enemy in an opposite direction from the town, as being the most sure course to take. Lt. Col. Williamson advised to march directly through the town, where there appeared to be no Indians, and the fires were yet burning.

There was no time or place for debates: Col. Crawford, with sixty followers retreated on the route that he had proposed by attempting to rush through the enemy; but they had no sooner got amongst the Indians than every man was killed or taken prisoner! Amongst the prisoners, were Col. Crawford, and Doct. Night, surgeon of the regiment.

Lt. Col. Williamson, with the remainder of the regiment, together with the wounded, set out at the same time that Crawford did, went through the town without losing a man, and by the help of good guides arrived at their homes in safety.

The next day after the engagement the Indians disposed of all their prisoners to the different tribes, except Col. Crawford and Doct. Night; but those unfortunate men were reserved for a more cruel destiny. A council was immediately held on Sandusky plains, consisting of all the Chiefs and warriors, ranged in their customary order, in a circular form; and Crawford and Night were brought forward and seated in the centre of the circle.

The council being opened, the Chiefs began to examine Crawford on various subjects relative to the war. At length they enquired who conducted the military operations of the American army on the Ohio and Susquehannah rivers, during the year before; and who had led that army against them with so much skill, and so uniform success? Crawford very honestly and without suspecting any harm from his reply, promptly answered that he was the man who had led his countrymen to victory, who had driven the enemy from the settlements, and by that means had procured a great degree of happiness to many of his fellow-citizens. Upon hearing this, a Chief, who had lost a son in the year before, in a battle where Colonel Crawford commanded, left his station in the council, stepped to Crawford, blacked his face, and at the same time told him that the next day he should be burnt.

The council was immediately dissolved on its
hearing the sentence from the Chief, and the prisoners were taken off the ground, and kept in cus-
tody through the night. Crawford now viewed his
fate as sealed; and despairing of ever returning
to his home or his country, only dreaded the tedi-
ousness of death, as commonly inflicted by the
savages, and earnestly hoped that he might be
despatched at a single blow.

Early the next morning, the Indians assembled
at the place of execution, and Crawford was led
to the post—the goal of savage torture, to which
he was fastened. The post was a stick of timber
placed firmly in the ground, having an arm framed
in at the top, and extending some six or eight feet
from it, like the arm of a sign post. A pile of wood
containing about two cords, lay a few feet from
the place where he stood, which he was informed
was to be kindled into a fire that would burn him
alive, as many had been burnt on the same spot,
who had been much less deserving than himself.

Gurty stood and composedly looked on the preparations that were making for the funeral of one
of his former playmates; a hero by whose side he
had fought; of a man whose valor had won laurels
which, if he could have returned, would have been
strewed upon his grave, by his grateful countrymen. Dreading the agony that he saw he was
about to feel, Crawford used every argument which
his perilous situation could suggest to prevail upon
Gurty to ransom him at any price, and deliver
him (as it was in his power,) from the savages,
and their torments. Gurty heard his prayers, and

expostulations, and saw his tears with indifference, and finally told the forsaken victim that he would not procure him a moment's respite, nor afford him the most trifling assistance.

The Col. was then bound, stripped naked and tied by his wrists to the arm, which extended horizontally from the post, in such a manner that his arms were extended over his head, with his feet just standing upon the ground. This being done, the savages placed the wood in a circle around him at the distance of a few feet, in order that his misery might be protracted to the greatest length, and then kindled it in a number of places at the same time. The flames arose and the scorching heat became almost insupportable. Again he prayed to Gurty in all the anguish of his torment, to rescue him from the fire, or shoot him dead upon the spot. A demoniac smile suffused the countenance of Gurty, while he calmly replied to the dying suppliant, that he had no pity for his sufferings; but that he was then satisfying that spirit of revenge, which for a long time he had hoped to have an opportunity to wreak upon him. Nature now almost exhausted from the intensity of the heat, he settled down a little, when a squaw threw coals of fire and embers upon him, which made him groan most piteously, while the whole camp rung with exultation. During the execution they manifested all the exstacy of a complete triumph. Poor Crawford soon died and was entirely consumed.

Thus ended the life of a patriot and hero, who had been an intimate with Gen. Washington, and who shared in an eminent degree the confidence

of that great, good man, to whom, in the time of
revolutionary perils, the sons of legitimate freedom
looked with a degree of faith in his mental re-
sources, unequalled in the history of the world.

That tragedy being ended, Doct. Night was informed that on the next day he should be burnt
in the same manner that his comrade Crawford
had been, at Lower Sandusky. Hiokatoo, who had
been a leading chief in the battle with, and in the
execution of Crawford, painted Doct. Night's face
black, and then bound and gave him up to two
able bodied Indians to conduct to the place of
execution.

They set off with him immediately, and travelled till towards evening, when they halted to encamp till morning. The afternoon had been very
rainy, and the storm still continued, which rendered it very difficult for the Indians to kindle a
fire. Night observing the difficulty under which
they labored, made them to understand by signs,
that if they would unbind him, he would assist
them.—They accordingly unloosed him, and he
soon succeeded in making a fire by the application
of small dry stuff which he was at considerable
trouble to procure. While the Indians were warming themselves, the Doct. continued to gather
wood to last through the night, and in doing this,
he found a club which he placed in a situation
from whence he could take it conveniently whenever an opportunity should present itself, in which
he could use it effectually. The Indians continued
warming, till at length the Doct. saw that they
had placed themselves in a favorable position for

the execution of his design, when, stimulated by the love of life, he cautiously took his club and at two blows knocked them both down. Determined to finish the work of death which he had so well begun, he drew one of their scalping knives, with which he beheaded and scalped them both! He then took a rifle, tomahawk, and some ammunition, and directed his course for home, where he arrived without having experienced any difficulty on his journey.

The next morning, the Indians took the track of their victim and his attendants, to go to Lower Sandusky, and there execute the sentence which they had pronounced upon him. But what was their surprise and disappointment, when they arrived at the place of encampment, where they found their trusty friends scalped and decapitated, and that their prisoner had made his escape?— Chagrined beyond measure, they immediately separated, and went in every direction in pursuit of their prey; but after having spent a number of days unsuccessfully, they gave up the chase, and returned to their encampment.*

In the time of the French war, in an engage-

*I have understood, (from unauthenticated sources however,) that soon after the revolutionary war, Doct. Night published a pamphlet, containing an account of the battle at Sandusky, and of his own sufferings. My information on this subject, was derived from a different quarter.

The subject of this narrative in giving the account of her last husband, Hiokatoo, referred us to Mr. George Jemison, who, (as it will be noticed) lived on her land a number of years, and who had frequently heard the old Chief relate the story of his life; particularly that part

ment that took place on the Ohio river, Hiokatoo took a British Col. by the name of Simon Canton, whom he carried to the Indian encampment. A council was held, and the Col. was sentenced to suffer death, by being tied on a wild colt, with his face towards its tail, and then having the colt turned loose to run where it pleased. He was accordingly tied on, and the colt let loose, agreeable to the sentence. The colt run two days and then returned with its rider yet alive. The Indians, thinking that he would never die in that way, took him off, and made him run the gauntlet three times; but in the last race a squaw knocked him down, and he was supposed to have been dead. He, however, recovered, and was sold for fifty dollars to a Frenchman, who sent him as a prisoner to Detroit. On the return of the Frenchman to Detroit, the Col. besought him to ransom him, and give, or set him at liberty, with so much warmth, and promised with so much solemnity, to reward him as one of the best of benefactors, if he would let him go, that the Frenchman took his word, and sent him home to his family. The Col. remembered his promise, and in a short time sent his deliverer which related to his military career. Mr. Jemison, on being enquired of, gave the foregoing account, partly from his own personal knowledge, and the remainder, from the account given by Hiokatoo.

Mr. Jemison was in the battle, was personally acquainted with Col. Crawford, and one that escaped with Lt. Col. Williamson. We have no doubt of the truth of the statement, and have therefore inserted the whole account, as an addition to the historical facts which are daily coming into a state of preservation, in relation to the American Revolution.   AUTHOR.

one hundred and fifty dollars, as a reward for his generosity.

Since the commencement of the revolutionary war, Hiokatoo has been in seventeen campaigns, four of which were in the Cherokee war. He was so great an enemy to the Cherokees, and so fully determined upon their subjugation, that on his march to their country, he raised his own army for those four campaigns, and commanded it; and also superintended its subsistence. In one of those campaigns, which continued two whole years without intermission, he attacked his enemies on the Mobile, drove them to the country of the Creek Nation, where he continued to harrass them, till being tired of war, he returned to his family. He brought home a great number of scalps, which he had taken from the enemy, and ever seemed to possess an unconquerable will that the Cherokees might be utterly destroyed. Towards the close of his last fighting in that country, he took two squaws, whom he sold on his way home for money to defray the expense of his journey.

Hiokatoo was about six feet four or five inches high, large boned, and rather inclined to leanness. He was very stout and active, for a man of his size, for it was said by himself and others, that he had never found an Indian who could keep up with him on a race, or throw him at wrestling. His eye was quick and penetrating; and his voice was of that harsh and powerful kind, which, amongst Indians, always commands attention. His health had been uniformly good. He never was confined by sickness, till he was attacked with the consumption, four years before his death. And, although he had, from his earliest days, been inured to almost constant fatigue, and exposure to the inclemency of the weather, in the open air, he seemed to lose the vigor of the prime of life only by the natural decay occasioned by old age.

✥◯✥◯✥

CHAPTER XII.

Her Troubles Renewed. John's Jealousy towards his brother Jesse. Circumstances attending the Murder of Jesse Jemison. Her Grief. His Funeral. Age—Filial Kindness, &c.

BEING now left a widow in my old age, to mourn the loss of a husband, who had treated me well, and with whom I had raised five children, and having suffered the loss of an affectionate son, I fondly fostered the hope that my melancholy vicissitudes had ended, and that the remainder of my time would be characterized by nothing unpropitious. My children, dutiful and kind, lived near me, and apparently nothing obstructed our happiness.

But a short time, however, elapsed after my husband's death, before my troubles were renewed with redoubled severity.

John's hands having been once stained in the blood of a brother, it was not strange that after his acquital, every person of his acquaintance should shun him, from a fear of his repeating upon them the same ceremony that he had practised upon Thomas. My son Jesse, went to Mt. Morris, a few miles from home, on business, in the winter after the death of his father; and it so happened that his brother John was there, who requested Jesse to come home with him. Jesse, fearing that John would commence a quarrel with him on the way, declined the invitation, and tarried over night.

From that time John conceived himself despised by Jesse, and was highly enraged at the treatment which he had received. Very little was said, however, and it all passed off, apparently, till sometime in the month of May, 1812, at which time Mr. Robert Whaley, who lived in the town of Castile, within four miles of me, came to my house early on Monday morning, to hire George Chongo, my son-in-law, and John and Jesse, to go that day and help him slide a quantity of boards from the top of the hill to the river, where he calculated to build a raft of them for market.

They all concluded to go with Mr. Whaley, and made ready as soon as possible. But before they set out I charged them not to drink any whiskey; for I was confident that if they did, they would surely have a quarrel in consequence of it. They went and worked till almost night, when a quarrel ensued between Chongo and Jesse, in consequence of the whiskey that they had drank through the day, which terminated in a battle, and Chongo got whipped.

When Jesse had got through with Chongo, he told Mr. Whaley that he would go home, and directly went off. He, however, went but a few rods before he stopped and lay down by the side of a log to wait, (as was supposed,) for company. John, as soon as Jesse was gone, went to Mr. Whaley, with his knife in his hand, and bade him jogo; (i.e. be gone,) at the same time telling him that Jesse was a bad man. Mr. Whaley, seeing that his countenance was changed, and that he was determined upon something desperate, was alarmed for his own safety, and turned towards home, leaving Chongo on the ground drunk, near to where Jesse had lain, who by this time had got up, and was advancing towards John. Mr. Whaley was soon out of hearing of them; but some of his workmen staid till it was dark. Jesse came up to John, and said to him, you want more whiskey, and more fighting, and after a few words went at him, to try in the first place to get away his knife. In this he did not succeed, and they parted. By this time the night had come on, and it was dark. Again they clenched and at length in their struggle they both fell. John, having his knife in his hand, came under, and in that situation gave Jesse a fatal stab with his knife, and repeated the blows till Jesse cried out, brother, you have killed me, quit his hold and settled back upon the ground.—Upon hearing this, John left him and came to Thomas' widow's house, told them that he had been fighting with their uncle, whom he had killed, and showed them his knife.

Next morning as soon as it was light, Thomas' and John's children came and told me that Jesse was dead in the woods, and also informed me how he came by his death. John soon followed them and informed me himself of all that had taken place between him and his brother, and seemed to be somewhat sorrowful for his conduct. You can better imagine what my feelings were than I can describe them. My darling son, my youngest child, him on whom I depended, was dead; and I in my old age left destitute of a helping hand!

As soon as it was consistent for me, I got Mr. George Jemison, (of whom I shall have occasion to speak,) to go with his sleigh to where Jesse was, and bring him home, a distance of 3 or 4 miles. My daughter Polly arrived at the fatal spot first: we got there soon after her; though I went the whole distance on foot. By this time, Chongo, (who was left on the ground drunk the night before,) had become sober and sensible of the great misfortune which had happened to our family.

I was overcome with grief at the sight of my murdered son, and so far lost the command of myself as to be almost frantic; and those who were present were obliged to hold me from going near him.

On examining the body it was found that it had received eighteen wounds so deep and large that it was believed that either of them would have proved mortal. The corpse was carried to my house, and kept till the Thursday following, when it was buried after the manner of burying white people.

Jesse was twenty-seven or eight years old when he was killed. His temper had been uniformly very mild and friendly; and he was inclined to copy after the white people; both in his manners and dress. Although he was naturally temperate, he occasionally became intoxicated; but never was quarrelsome or mischievous. With the white people he was intimate, and learned from them their habits of industry, which he was fond of practising, especially when my comfort demanded his labor. As I have observed, it is the custom amongst the Indians, for the women to perform all the labor in, and out of doors, and I had the whole to do, with the help of my daughters, till Jesse arrived to a sufficient age to assist us. He was disposed to labor in the cornfield, to chop my wood, milk my cows, and attend to any kind of business that would make my task the lighter. On the account of his having been my youngest child, and so willing to help me, I am sensible that I loved him better than I did either of my other children. After he began to understand my situation, and the means of rendering it more easy, I never wanted for any thing that was in his power to bestow; but since his death, as I have had all my labor to perform alone, I have constantly seen hard times.

Jesse shunned the company of his brothers, and the Indians generally, and never attended their frolics; and it was supposed that this, together with my partiality for him, were the causes which excited in John so great a degree of envy, that nothing short of death would satisfy it.

❖◉❖◉❖

CHAPTER XIII.

Mrs. Jemison is informed that she has a Cousin in the Neighborhood, by the name of George Jemison. His Poverty. Her Kindness. His Ingratitude. Her Trouble from Land Speculation. Her Cousin moves off.

A YEAR or two before the death of my husband, Capt. H. Jones sent me word, that a cousin of mine was then living in Leicester, (a few miles from Gardow,) by the name of George Jemison, and as he was very poor, thought it advisable for me to go and see him, and take him home to live with me on my land. My Indian friends were pleased to hear that one of my relatives was so near, and also advised me to send for him and his family immediately. I accordingly had him and his family moved into one of my houses, in the month of March, 1810.

He said that he was my father's brother's son— that his father did not leave Europe, till after the French war in America, and that when he did come over, he settled in Pennsylvania, where he died. George had no personal knowledge of my father; but from information, was confident that the relationship which he claimed between himself and me, actually existed. Although I had never before heard of my father having had but one brother, (him who was killed at Fort Necessity,) yet I knew that he might have had others, and, as the story of George carried with it a probability that it was true, I received him as a kinsman, and treated him with every degree of friendship which his situation demanded.*

I found that he was destitute of the means of subsistence, and in debt to the amount of seventy dollars, without the ability to pay one cent. He had no cow, and finally, was completely poor. I paid

*Mrs. Jemison is now confident that George Jemison is not her cousin, and thinks that he claimed the relationship, only to gain assistance: But the old gentleman, who is now living, is certain that his and her father were brothers, as before stated.

his debts to the amount of seventy-two dollars, and bought him a cow, for which I paid twenty dollars, and a sow and pigs, that I paid eight dollars for. I also paid sixteen dollars for pork that I gave him, and furnished him with other provisions and furniture; so that his family was comfortable. As he was destitute of a team, I furnished him with one, and also supplied him with tools for farming. In addition to all this, I let him have one of Thomas' cows, for two seasons.

My only object in mentioning his poverty, and the articles with which I supplied him, is to show how ungrateful a person can be for favors, and how soon a kind benefactor will, to all appearance, be forgotten.

Thus furnished with the necessary implements of husbandry, a good team, and as much land as he could till, he commenced farming on my flats, and for some time labored well. At length, however, he got an idea that if he could become the owner of a part of my reservation, he could live more easy, and certainly be more rich, and accordingly set himself about laying a plan to obtain it, in the easiest manner possible.

I supported Jemison and his family eight years, and probably should have continued to have done so to this day, had it not been for the occurrence of the following circumstance.

When he had lived with me some six or seven years, a friend of mine told me that as Jemison was my cousin, and very poor, I ought to give him a piece of land that he might have something whereon to live, that he would call his own.

My friend and Jemison were then together at my house, prepared to complete a bargain. I asked how much land he wanted? Jemison said that he should be glad to receive his old field (as he called it) containing about fourteen acres, and a new one that contained twenty-six.

I observed to them that as I was incapable of transacting business of that nature, I would wait till Mr. Thomas Clute, (a neighbor on whom I depended,) should return from Albany, before I should do any thing about it. To this Jemison replied that if I waited till Mr. Clute returned, he should not get the land at all, and appeared very anxious to have the business closed without delay. On my part, I felt disposed to give him some land, but knowing my ignorance of writing, feared to do it alone, lest they might include as much land as they pleased, without my knowledge.

They then read the deed which my friend had prepared before he came from home, describing a piece of land by certain bounds that were a specified number of chains and links from each other. Not understanding the length of a chain or link, I described the bounds of a piece of land that I intended Jemison should have, which they said was just the same that the deed contained and no more. I told them that the deed must not include a lot that was called the Steele place, and they assured me that it did not. Upon this, putting confidence in them both, I signed the deed to George Jemison, containing, and conveying to him as I supposed, forty acres of land. The deed being completed they charged me never to mention the bargain which I had then made to any person; because if I did, they said it would spoil the contract. The whole matter was afterwards disclosed; when it was found that that deed instead of containing only forty acres, contained four hundred, and that one half of it actually belonged to my friend, as it had been given to him by Jemison as a reward for his trouble in procuring the deed, in the fraudulent manner above mentioned.

My friend, however, by the advice of some well disposed people, awhile afterwards gave up his claim; but Jemison held his till he sold it for a trifle to a gentleman in the south part of Genesee county.

Sometime after the death of my son Thomas, one of his sons went to Jemison to get the cow that I had let him have two years; but Jemison refused to let her go, and struck the boy so violent a blow as to almost kill him. Jemison then run to Jellis Clute, Esq. to procure a warrant to take the boy; but Young King, an Indian Chief, went down to Squawky hill to Esq. Clute's, and settled the affair by Jemison's agreeing never to use that club again. Having satisfactorily found out the friendly disposition of my cousin towards me, I got him off my premises as soon as possible.

❖◯❖◯❖

CHAPTER XIV.

Another Family Affliction. Her son John's Occupation. He goes to Buffalo—Returns. Great Slide by him considered Ominous—Trouble, &c. He goes to Squawky Hill— Quarrels—Is murdered by two Indians. His Funeral— Mourners, &c. His Disposition. Ominous Dream. Black

*Chief's Advice, &c. His Widows and Family. His Age.
His Murderers flee. Her Advice to them. They set out
to leave their Country. Their Uncle's Speech to them on
parting. They return. Jack proposes to Doctor to kill
each other. Doctor's Speech in Reply. Jack's Suicide.
Doctor's Death.*

TROUBLE seldom comes single. While George
Jemison was busily engaged in his pursuit of wealth
at my expence, another event of a much more serious nature occurred, which added greatly to my
afflictions, and consequently destroyed, at least a
part of the happiness that I had anticipated was
laid up in the archives of Providence, to be dis-
pensed on my old age.

My son John, was a doctor, considerably celebrated amongst the Indians of various tribes, for
his skill in curing their diseases, by the administration of roots and herbs, which he gathered in
the forests, and other places where they had been
planted by the hand of nature.

In the month of April, or first of May, 1817, he
was called upon to go to Buffalo, Cattaraugus and
Allegany, to cure some who were sick. He went,
and was absent about two months. When he returned, he observed the Great Slide of the bank of
Genesee river, a short distance above my house,
which had taken place during his absence; and conceiving that circumstance to be ominous of his own
death, called at his sister Nancy's, told her that
he should live but a few days, and wept bitterly
at the near approach of his dissolution. Nancy
endeavored to persuade him that his trouble was
imaginary, and that he ought not to be affected by

a fancy which was visionary. Her arguments were ineffectual, and afforded no alleviation to his mental sufferings. From his sister's, he went to his own house, where he stayed only two nights, and then went to Squawky Hill to procure money, with which to purchase flour for the use of his family.

While at Squawky Hill he got into the company of two Squawky Hill Indians, whose names were Doctor and Jack, with whom he drank freely, and in the afternoon had a desperate quarrel, in which his opponents, (as it was afterwards understood,) agreed to kill him. The quarrel ended, and each appeared to be friendly. John bought some spirits, of which they all drank, and then set out for home. John and an Allegany Indian were on horseback, and Doctor and Jack were on foot. It was dark when they set out. They had not proceeded far, when Doctor and Jack commenced another quarrel with John, clenched and dragged him off his horse, and then with a stone gave him so severe a blow on his head, that some of his brains were discharged from the wound. The Allegany Indian, fearing that his turn would come next, fled for safety as fast as possible.

John recovered a little from the shock he had received, and endeavored to get to an old hut that stood near; but they caught him, and with an axe cut his throat, and beat out his brains, so that when he was found the contents of his skull were lying on his arms.

Some squaws, who heard the uproar, ran to find out the cause of it; but before they had time to offer their assistance, the murderers drove them into a house, and threatened to take their lives if they did not stay there, or if they made any noise.

Next morning, Esq. Clute sent me word that John was dead, and also informed me of the means by which his life was taken. A number of people went from Gardow to where the body lay, and Doct. Levi Brundridge brought it up home, where the funeral was attended after the manner of the white people. Mr. Benjamin Luther, and Mr. William Wiles, preached a sermon, and performed the funeral services; and myself and family followed the corpse to the grave as mourners. I had now buried my three sons, who had been snatched from me by the hands of violence, when I least expected it.

Although John had taken the life of his two brothers, and caused me unspeakable trouble and grief, his death made a solemn impression upon my mind, and seemed, in addition to my former misfortunes, enough to bring down my grey hairs with sorrow to the grave. Yet, on a second thought, I could not mourn for him as I had for my other sons, because I knew that his death was just, and what he had deserved for a long time, from the hand of justice.

John's vices were so great and so aggravated, that I have nothing to say in his favor: yet, as a mother, I pitied him while he lived, and have ever felt a great degree of sorrow for him, because of his bad conduct.

From his childhood, he carried something in his features indicative of an evil disposition, that would result in the perpetration of enormities of

some kind; and it was the opinion and saying of
Ebenezer Allen, that he would be a bad man, and
be guilty of some crime deserving of death. There
is no doubt but what the thoughts of murder ran-
kled in his breast, and disturbed his mind even
in his sleep; for he dreamed that he had killed
Thomas for a trifling offence, and thereby forfeited his own life. Alarmed at the revelation, and
fearing that he might in some unguarded moment
destroy his brother, he went to the Black Chief, to
whom he told the dream, and expressed his fears
that the vision would be verified. Having related
the dream, together with his feelings on the subject, he asked for the best advice that his old friend
was capable of giving, to prevent so sad an event.
The Black Chief, with his usual promptitude, told
him, that from the nature of the dream, he was
fearful that something serious would take place
between him and Thomas; and advised him by
all means to govern his temper, and avoid any
quarrel which in future he might see arising, especially if Thomas was a party. John, however,
did not keep the good counsel of the Chief; for
soon after he killed Thomas, as I have related.

John left two wives with whom he had lived at
the same time, and raised nine children. His widows are now living at Caneadea with their father,
and keep their children with, and near them. His
children are tolerably white, and have got light
colored hair. John died about the last day of June,
1817, aged 54 years.

Doctor and Jack having finished their murderous design, fled before they could be apprehended,

and lay six weeks in the woods back of Canisteo. They then returned and sent me some wampum by Chongo, (my son-in-law,) and Sun-ge-waw (that is Big Kettle) expecting that I would pardon them, and suffer them to live as they had done with their tribe. I however, would not accept their wampum, but returned it with a request, that, rather than have them killed, they would run away and keep out of danger.

On their receiving back the wampum, they took my advice, and prepared to leave their country and people immediately. Their relatives accompanied them a short distance on their journey, and when about to part, their old uncle, the Tall Chief, addressed them in the following pathetic and sentimental speech:

"Friends, hear my voice!—When the Great Spirit made Indians, he made them all good, and gave them good corn-fields; good rivers, well stored with fish; good forests, filled with game and good bows and arrows. But very soon each wanted more than his share, and Indians quarrelled with Indians, and some were killed, and others were wounded. Then the Great Spirit made a very good word, and put it in every Indians breast, to tell us when we have done good, or when we have done bad; and that word has never told a lie.

"Friends! whenever you have stole, or got drunk, or lied, that good word has told you that you were bad Indians, and made you afraid of good Indians; and made you ashamed and look down.

"Friends! your crime is greater than all those: —you have killed an Indian in a time of peace;

and made the wind hear his groans, and the earth drink his blood. You are bad Indians! Yes, you are very bad Indians; and what can you do? If you go into the woods to live alone, the ghost of John Jemison will follow you, crying, blood! blood! and will give you no peace! If you go to the land of your nation, there that ghost will attend you, and say to your relatives, see my murderers! If you plant, it will blast your corn; if you hunt, it will scare your game; and when you are asleep, its groans, and the sight of an avenging tomahawk, will awake you! What can you do? Deserving of death, you cannot live here; and to fly from your country, to leave all your relatives, and to abandon all that you have known to be pleasant and dear, must be keener than an arrow, more bitter than gall, more terrible than death! And how must we feel?—Your path will be muddy; the woods will be dark; the lightnings will glance down the trees by your side, and you will start at every sound! peace has left you, and you must be wretched.

"Friends, hear me, and take my advice. Return with us to your homes. Offer to the Great Spirit your best wampum, and try to be good Indians! And, if those whom you have bereaved shall claim your lives as their only satisfaction, surrender them cheerfully, and die like good Indians. And—"Here Jack, highly incensed, interrupted the old man, and bade him stop speaking or he would take his life. Affrighted at the appearance of so much desperation, the company hastened towards home, and left Doctor and Jack to consult their own feelings.

As soon as they were alone, Jack said to Doctor, "I had rather die here, than leave my country and friends! Put the muzzle of your rifle into my mouth, and I will put the muzzle of mine into yours, and at a given signal we will discharge them, and rid ourselves at once of all the troubles under which we now labor, and satisfy the claims which justice holds against us."

Doctor heard the proposition, and after a moment's pause, made the following reply:—"I am as sensible as you can be of the unhappy situation in which we have placed ourselves. We are bad Indians. We have forfeited our lives, and must expect in some way to atone for our crime: but, because we are bad and miserable, shall we make ourselves worse? If we were now innocent, and in a calm reflecting moment should kill ourselves, that act would make us bad, and deprive us of our share of the good hunting in the land where our fathers have gone! What would Little Beard* say to us on our arrival at his cabin? He would say, 'Bad Indians! Cowards! You were afraid to wait till we wanted your help! Go (Jogo) to where snakes will lie in your path; where the panthers will starve you, by devouring the venison; and where you will be naked and suffer with the cold! Jogo, (go,) none but the brave and good Indians live here!' I cannot think of performing an act that will add to my wretchedness. It is hard enough for me to suffer here, and have good hunting hereafter—worse to lose the whole."

Upon this, Jack withdrew his proposal. They

*Little Beard was a Chief who died in 1806.

MARY JEMISON

went on about two miles, and then turned about
and came home. Guilty and uneasy, they lurked
about Squawky Hill near a fortnight, and then
went to Cattaraugus, and were gone six weeks.
When they came back, Jack's wife earnestly requested him to remove his family to Tonnewonta;
but he remonstrated against her project, and utterly declined going. His wife and family, however, tired of the tumult by which they were
surrounded, packed up their effects in spite of
what he could say, and went off.

Jack deliberated a short time upon the proper
course for himself to pursue, and finally, rather
than leave his old home, he ate a large quantity
of muskrat root, and died in 10 or 12 hours. His
family being immediately notified of his death,
returned to attend the burial, and is yet living at
Squawky Hill.

Nothing was ever done with Doctor, who continued to live quietly at Squawky Hill till sometime
in the year 1819, when he died of Consumption.

❖◉❖◉❖

CHAPTER XV.

*Micah Brooks, Esq. volunteers to get the Title to her
Land confirmed to herself. She is Naturalized. Great
Council of Chiefs, &c. in Sept. 1823. She Disposes of
her Reservation. Reserves a Tract 2 miles long, and
1 mile wide, &c. The Consideration how Paid, &c.*

In 1816, Micah Brooks, Esq. of Bloomfield,
Ontario county, was recommended to me (as it
was said) by a Mr. Ingles, to be a man of candor,

[119]

honesty and integrity, who would by no means cheat me out of a cent. Mr. Brooks soon after, came to my house and informed me that he was disposed to assist me in regard to my land, by procuring a legislative act that would invest me with full power to dispose of it for my own benefit, and give as ample a title as could be given by any citizen of the state. He observed that as it was then situated, it was of but little value, because it was not in my power to dispose of it, let my necessities be ever so great. He then proposed to take the agency of the business upon himself, and to get the title of one half of my reservation vested in me personally, upon the condition that, as a reward for his services, I would give him the other half.

I sent for my son John, who on being consulted, objected to my going into any bargain with Mr. Brooks, without the advice and consent of Mr. Thomas Clute, who then lived on my land and near me. Mr. Clute was accordingly called on, to whom Mr. Brooks repeated his former statement, and added, that he would get an act passed in the Congress of the United States, that would invest me with all the rights and immunities of a citizen, so far as it respected my property. Mr. Clute, suspecting that some plan was in operation that would deprive me of my possessions, advised me to have nothing to say on the subject to Mr. Brooks, till I had seen Esquire Clute, of Squawky Hill. Soon after this Thomas Clute saw Esq. Clute, who informed him that the petition for my naturalization would be presented to the Legislature of this

State, instead of being sent to Congress; and that the object would succeed to his and my satisfaction. Mr. Clute then observed to his brother, Esq. Clute, that as the sale of Indian lands, which had been reserved, belonged exclusively to the United States, an act of the Legislature of New-York could have no effect in securing to me a title to my reservation, or in depriving me of my property. They finally agreed that I should sign a petition to Congress, praying for my naturalization, and for the confirmation of the title of my land to me, my heirs, &c.

Mr. Brooks came with the petition: I signed it, and it was witnessed by Thomas Clute, and two others, and then returned to Mr. Brooks, who presented it to the Legislature of this state at its session in the winter of 1816–17. On the 19th of April, 1817, an act was passed for my naturalization, and ratifying and confirming the title of my land, agreeable to the tenor of the petition, which act Mr. Brooks presented to me on the first day of May following.

Thomas Clute having examined the law, told me that it would probably answer, though it was not according to the agreement made by Mr. Brooks, and Esq. Clute and himself, for me. I then executed to Micah Brooks and Jellis Clute, a deed of all my land lying east of the picket line on the Gardow reservation, containing about 7000 acres.

It is proper in this place to observe, in relation to Mr. Thomas Clute, that my son John, a few months before his death, advised me to take him for my guardian, (as I had become old and incapable of managing my property,) and to compensate him for his trouble by giving him a lot of land on the west side of my reservation where he should choose it. I accordingly took my son's advice, and Mr. Clute has ever since been faithful and honest in all his advice and dealings with, and for, myself and family.

In the month of August, 1817, Mr. Brooks and Esq. Clute again came to me with a request that I would give them a lease of the land which I had already deeded to them, together with the other part of my reservation, excepting and reserving to myself only about 4000 acres.

At this time I informed Thomas Clute of what John had advised, and recommended me to do, and that I had consulted my daughters on the subject, who had approved of the measure. He readily agreed to assist me; whereupon I told him he was entitled to a lot of land, and might select as John had mentioned. He accordingly at that time took such a piece as he chose, and the same has ever since been reserved for him in all the land contracts which I have made.

On the 24th of August, 1817, I leased to Micah Brooks and Jellis Clute, the whole of my original reservation, except 4000 acres, and Thomas Clute's lot. Finding their title still incomplete, on account of the United States government and Seneca Chiefs not having sanctioned my acts, they solicited me to renew the contract, and have the conveyance made to them in such a manner as that they should thereby be constituted sole proprietors of the soil.

In the winter of 1822–3, I agreed with them, that if they would get the chiefs of our nation, and a United States Commissioner of Indian Lands, to meet in council at Moscow, Livingston county, N. Y. and there concur in my agreement, that I would sell to them all my right and title to the Gardow reservation, with the exception of a tract for my own benefit, two miles long, and one mile wide, lying on the river where I should choose it; and also reserving Thomas Clute's lot. This arrangement was agreed upon, and the council assembled at the place appointed, on the 3d or 4th day of September, 1823.

That council consisted of Major Carrol, who had been appointed by the President to dispose of my lands, Judge Howell and N. Gorham, of Canandaigua, (who acted in concert with Maj. Carrol,) Jasper Parrish, Indian Agent, Horatio Jones, Interpreter, and a great number of Chiefs.

The bargain was assented to unanimously, and a deed given to H. B. Gibson, Micah Brooks and Jellis Clute, of the whole Gardow tract, excepting the last mentioned reservations, which was signed by myself and upwards of twenty Chiefs.

The land which I now own, is bounded as follows:—Beginning at the center of the Great Slide* and running west one mile, thence north two miles, thence east about one mile to Genesee river, thence

*The Great Slide of the bank of Genesee river is a curiosity worthy of the attention of the traveller. In the month of May, 1817, a portion of land thickly covered with timber, situated at the upper end of the Gardow flats, on the west side of the river, all of a sudden gave way, and with a tremendous crash, slid into the bed of

south on the west bank of Genesee river to the place of beginning.

In consideration of the above sale, the purchasers have bound themselves, their heirs, assigns, &c. to pay to me, my heirs or successors, three hundred dollars a year forever.

Whenever the land which I have reserved, shall be sold, the income of it is to be equally divided amongst the members of the Seneca nation, without any reference to tribes or families.

✵◯✵◯✵

CHAPTER XVI.

Conclusion. Review of her Life. Reflections on the loss of Liberty. Care she took to preserve her Health. Indians' abstemiousness in Drinking, after the French War. Care of their Lives, &c. General use of Spirits. Her natural Strength. Purchase of her first Cow. Means by which she has been supplied with Food. Suspicions of her having been a Witch. Her Constancy. Number of Children. Number Living. Their Residence. Closing Reflection.

WHEN I review my life, the privations that I have suffered, the hardships I have endured, the vicissitudes I have passed, and the complete revolution that I have experienced in my manner of living; when I consider my reduction from a civilized to a savage state, and the various steps by which that process has been effected, and that my

the river, which it so completely filled, that the stream formed a new passage on the east side of it, where it continues to run, without overflowing the slide. This slide, as it now lies, contains 22 acres, and has a considerable share of the timber that formerly covered it, still standing erect upon it, and growing.

life has been prolonged, and my health and reason spared, it seems a miracle that I am unable to account for, and is a tragical medley that I hope will never be repeated.

The bare loss of liberty is but a mere trifle when compared with the circumstances that necessarily attend, and are inseparably connected with it. It is the recollection of what we once were, of the friends, the home, and the pleasures that we have left or lost; the anticipation of misery, the appearance of wretchedness, the anxiety for freedom, the hope of release, the devising of means of escaping, and the vigilance with which we watch our keepers, that constitute the nauseous dregs of the bitter cup of slavery. I am sensible, however, that no one can pass from a state of freedom to that of slavery, and in the last situation rest perfectly contented; but as every one knows that great exertions of the mind tend directly to debilitate the body, it will appear obvious that we ought, when confined, to exert all our faculties to promote our present comfort, and let future days provide their own sacrifices. In regard to ourselves, just as we feel, we are.

For the preservation of my life to the present time I am indebted to an excellent constitution, with which I have been blessed in as great a degree as any other person. After I arrived to years of understanding, the care of my own health was one of my principal studies; and by avoiding exposures to wet and cold, by temperance in eating, abstaining from the use of spirits, and shunning the excesses to which I was frequently exposed, I effected my object beyond what I expected. I have never once been sick till within a year or two, only as I have related.

Spirits and tobacco I have never used, and I have never once attended an Indian frolic. When I was taken prisoner, and for sometime after that, spirits was not known; and when it was first introduced, it was in small quantities, and used only by the Indians; so that it was a long time before the Indian women begun to even taste it.

After the French war, for a number of years, it was the practice of the Indians of our tribe to send to Niagara and get two or three kegs of rum, (in all six or eight gallons,) and hold a frolic as long as it lasted. When the rum was brought to the town, all the Indians collected, and before a drop was drank, gave all their knives, tomahawks, guns, and other instruments of war, to one Indian, whose business it was to bury them in a private place, keep them concealed, and remain perfectly sober till the frolic was ended. Having thus divested themselves, they commenced drinking, and continued their frolic till every drop was consumed. If any of them became quarrelsome, or got to fighting, those who were sober enough bound them upon the ground, where they were obliged to lie till they got sober, and then were unbound. When the fumes of the spirits had left the company, the sober Indian returned to each the instruments with which they had entrusted him, and all went home satisfied. A frolic of that kind was held but once a year, and that at the time the Indians quit their hunting, and come in with their deer-skins.

In those frolics the women never participated. Soon after the revolutionary war, however, spirits became common in our tribe, and has been used indiscriminately by both sexes; though there are not so frequent instances of intoxication amongst the squaws as amongst the Indians.

To the introduction and use of that baneful article, which has made such devastation in our tribes, and threatens the extinction of our people, (the Indians,) I can with the greatest propriety impute the whole of my misfortune in losing my three sons. But as I have before observed, not even the love of life will restrain an Indian from sipping the poison that he knows will destroy him. The voice of nature, the rebukes of reason, the advice of parents, the expostulations of friends, and the numerous instances of sudden death, are all insufficient to reclaim an Indian, who has once experienced the exhilarating and inebriating effects of spirits, from seeking his grave in the bottom of his bottle!

My strength has been great for a woman of my size, otherwise I must long ago have died under the burdens which I was obliged to carry. I learned to carry loads on my back, in a strap placed across my forehead, soon after my captivity; and continue to carry in the same way. Upwards of thirty years ago, with the help of my young children, I backed all the boards that were used about my house from Allen's mill at the outlet of Silver Lake, a distance of five miles. I have planted, hoed, and harvested corn every season but one since I was taken prisoner. Even this present fall (1823)

I have husked my corn and backed it into the house.

The first cow that I ever owned, I bought of a squaw sometime after the revolution. It had been stolen from the enemy. I had owned it but a few days when it fell into a hole, and almost died before we could get it out. After this, the squaw wanted to be recanted, but as I would not give up the cow, I gave her money enough to make, when added to the sum which I paid her at first, thirty-five dollars. Cows were plenty on the Ohio, when I lived there, and of good quality.

For provisions I have never suffered since I came upon the flats; nor have I ever been in debt to any other hands than my own for the plenty that I have shared.

My vices, that have been suspected, have been but few. It was believed for a long time, by some of our people, that I was a great witch; but they were unable to prove my guilt, and consequently I escaped the certain doom of those who are convicted of that crime, which, by Indians, is considered as heinous as murder. Some of my children had light brown hair, and tolerable fair skin, which used to make some say that I stole them; yet as I was ever conscious of my own constancy, I never thought that any one really believed that I was guilty of adultery.

I have been the mother of eight children; three of whom are now living, and I have at this time thirty-nine grand children, and fourteen great-grand children, all living in the neighborhood of Genesee River, and at Buffalo.

I live in my own house, and on my own land, with my youngest daughter, Polly, who is married to George Chongo, and has three children.

My daughter Nancy, who is married to Billy Green, lives about 80 rods south of my house, and has seven children.

My other daughter, Betsey, is married to John Green, has seven children, and resides 80 rods north of my house.

Thus situated in the midst of my children, I expect I shall soon leave the world, and make room for the rising generation. I feel the weight of years with which I am loaded, and am sensible of my daily failure in seeing, hearing and strength; but my only anxiety is for my family. If my family will live happily, and I can be exempted from trouble while I have to stay, I feel as though I could lay down in peace a life that has been checked in almost every hour, with troubles of a deeper dye, than are commonly experienced by mortals.

APPENDIX

❖◯❖◯❖

IT is to be regretted that an event of so tragical a nature as the following, should have escaped the pens of American Historians, and have been suffered to slide down the current of time, to the verge of oblivion, without having been snatched almost from the vortex of forgetfulness, and placed on the faithful page, as a memorial of premeditated cruelties, which, in former times, were practised upon the white people, by the North American Savages.

Modern History, perhaps, cannot furnish a parallel so atrocious in design and execution, as the one before us, and it may be questioned, even if the history of ancient times, when men fought hand to hand, and disgraced their nature by inventing engines of torture, can more than produce its equal.

It will be observed in the preceding narrative, that the affair at the Devil's Hole is said to have happened in November, 1759. That Mrs. Jemison arrived at Genesee about that time, is rendered certain from a number of circumstances; and that a battle was fought on the Niagara in Nov. 1759, in which two prisoners and some oxen were taken, and brought to Genesee, as she has stated, is altogether probable. But it is equally certain that the event which is the subject of this article, did not take place till the year 1763.

In the time of the French war, the neighborhood of Forts Niagara and Sclusser, (or Schlosser, as it was formerly written,) on the Niagara river, was a general battle-ground, and for this reason, Mrs. Jemison's memory ought not to be charged with treachery, for not having been able to distinguish accurately, after the lapse of sixty years, between the circumstances of one engagement and those of another. She resided on the Genesee at the time when the warriors of that tribe marched off to assist in laying the ambush at the Devil's Hole; and no one will doubt her having heard them rehearse the story of the event of that nefarious campaign, after they returned.

Chronology and history concur in stating that Fort Niagara was taken from the French, by the British, and that Gen. Prideaux was killed on the 25th of July, 1759.

Having obtained from Mrs. Jemison a kind of introduction to the story, I concluded that if it yet remained possible to procure a correct account of the circumstances which led to and attended that transaction, it would be highly gratifying to the American public. I accordingly directed a letter to Mr. Linus S. Everett, of Buffalo, whose ministerial labor, I well knew, frequently called him to Lewiston, requesting him to furnish me with a particular account of the destruction of the British, at the time and place before mentioned. He obligingly complied with my request, and gave me the result of his inquiries on that subject, in the following letter:—

Copy of a letter from Mr. Linus S. Everett, dated Fort Sclusser, 29th December, 1823.

Respected and dear friend,

I hasten, with much pleasure, to comply with your request, in regard to the affair at the Devil's Hole. I have often wondered that no authentic account has ever been given of that bloody and tragical scene.

I have made all the inquiries that appear to be of any use, and proceed to give you the result.

At this place, (Fort Sclusser,) an old gentleman now resides, to whom I am indebted for the best account of the affair that can be easily obtained. His name is Jesse Ware—his age about 74. Although he was not a resident of this part of the country at the time of the event, yet from his intimate acquaintance with one of the survivors, he is able to give much information, which otherwise could not be obtained.

The account that he gives is as follows:—In July, 1759, the British, under Sir William Johnston, took possession of Forts Niagara and Sclusser, which had before been in the hands of the French. At this time, the Seneca Indians, (which were a numerous and powerful nation,) were hostile to the British, and warmly allied to the French. These two posts, (viz.) Niagara and Sclusser, were of great importance to the British, on the account of affording the means of communication with the posts above, or on the upper lakes. In 1760, a contract was made between Sir William Johnston

and a Mr. Stedman, to construct a portage road
from Queenston landing to Fort Sclusser, a distance of eight miles, in order to facilitate the trans-
portation of provision, ammunition, &c. from one
place to the other. In conformity to this agreement, on the 20th of June, 1763, Stedman had
completed his road, and appeared at Queenston
Landing, (now Lewiston,) with twenty-five portage wagons, and one hundred horses and oxen, to
transport to Fort Sclusser the king's stores.

At this time Sir William Johnston was suspi-
cious of the intentions of the Senecas; for after
the surrender of the forts by the French, they had
appeared uneasy and hostile. In order to prevent
the teams, drivers and goods, receiving injury, he
detached 300 troops to guard them across the portage. The teams, under this escort, started from
Queenston landing—Stedman, who had the charge
of the whole, was on horseback, and rode between
the troops and teams; all the troops being in front.
On a small hill near the Devil's Hole, at that time,
was a redoubt of twelve men, which served as a
kind of guard on ordinary occasions, against the
depredations of the savages. "On the arrival of
the troops and teams at the Devil's Hole," says
a manuscript in the hands of my informant, "the
sachems, chiefs and warriors of the Seneca Indians,
sallied from the adjoining woods, by thousands,
(where they had been concealed for some time before, for that nefarious purpose,) and falling upon
the troops, teams and drivers, and the guard of
twelve men before mentioned, they killed all the
men but three on the spot, or by driving them, to-

gether with the teams, down the precipice, which was about seventy or eighty feet! The Indians seized Stedman's horse by the bridle, while he was on him, designing, no doubt, to make his sufferings more lasting than that of his companions: but while the bloody scene was acting, the attention of the Indian who held the horse of Stedman being arrested, he cut the reins of his bridle — clapped spurs to his horse, and rode over the dead and dying, into the adjacent woods, without receiving injury from the enemy's firing. Thus he escaped; and besides him two others — one a drummer, who fell among the trees, was caught by his drum strap, and escaped unhurt; the other, one who fell down the precipice and broke his thigh, but crawled to the landing or garrison down the river." The following September, the Indians gave Stedman a piece of land, as a reward for his bravery.

With sentiments of respect, I remain, sir, your sincere friend,   L. S. EVERETT.

Mr. J. E. Seaver.

❖◯❖◯❖

A particular account of General Sullivan's Expedition against the Indians, in the western part of the State of New-York, in 1779.

IT has been thought expedient to publish in this volume, the following account of Gen. Sullivan's expedition, in addition to the facts related by Mrs. Jemison, of the barbarities which were perpetrated upon Lieut. Boyd, and two others, who were taken, and who formed a part of his army, &c. A detailed account of this expedition has never been in the hands of the public; and as it is now produced from a source deserving implicit credit, it is presumed that it will be received with satisfaction. John Salmon, Esq. to whom we are happy to acknowledge our indebtedness for the subjoined account, is an old gentleman of respectability and good standing in society; and is at this time a resident in the town of Groveland, Livingston county, New-York. He was a hero in the American war for independence; fought in the battles of his country under the celebrated Morgan; survived the blast of British oppression; and now, in the decline of life, sits under his own well earned vine and fig-tree, near the grave of his unfortunate countrymen, who fell gloriously, while fighting the ruthless savages, under the command of the gallant Boyd.

In the autumn after the battle of Monmouth, (1778,) Morgan's riflemen, to which corps I belonged, marched to Schoharie, in the state of New-York, and there went into winter quarters. The company to which I was attached, was commanded by Capt. Michael Simpson; and Thomas Boyd, of Northumberland county, Pennsylvania, was our Lieutenant.

In the following spring, our corps, together with the whole body of troops under the command of Gen. Clinton, to the amount of about 1500, embarked in boats at Schenectady, and ascended the Mohawk as far as German Flats. Thence we took a direction to Otsego lake, descended the Susquehanna, and without any remarkable occurrence, arrived at Tioga Point, where our troops united with an army of 1500 men under the command of Gen. Sullivan, who had marched through a part of New-Jersey, and had reached that place by the way of Wyoming, some days before us.

That part of the army under Gen. Sullivan, had, on their arrival at Tioga Point, found the Indians in some force there, with whom they had had some unimportant skirmishes before our arrival. Upon the junction of these two bodies of troops, Gen. Sullivan assumed the command of the whole, and proceeded up the Tioga. When within a few miles of the place now called Newtown, we were met by a body of Indians, and a number of troops well known in those times by the name of Butler's Rangers, who had thrown up, hastily, a breastwork of logs, trees, &c. They were, however, easily driven from their works, with considerable loss on their part, and without any injury to our troops. The enemy fled with so much precipitation, that they left behind them some stores and camp equippage. They retreated but a short distance before they made a stand, and built another breastwork of considerable length, in the woods, near a small opening. Sullivan was soon apprized of their situation, divided his army, and attempted to surround, by sending one half to the right and the other to the left, with directions to meet on the opposite side of the enemies. In order to prevent their retreating, he directed bombshells to be thrown over them, which was done: but on the shells bursting, the Indians suspected that a powerful army had opened a heavy fire upon them on that side, and fled with the utmost precipitation through one wing of the surrounding army. A great number of the enemy were killed, and our army suffered considerably.

The Indians having, in this manner, escaped, they went up the river to a place called the Narrows, where they were attacked by our men, who killed them in great numbers, so that the sides of the rocks next the river appeared as though blood had been poured on them by pailfuls. The Indians threw their dead into the river, and escaped the best way they could.

From Newtown our army went directly to the head of the Seneca lake; thence down that lake to its mouth, where we found the Indian village at that place evacuated, except by a single inhabitant—a male child about seven or eight years of age, who was found asleep in one of the Indian huts. Its fate I have never ascertained. It was taken into the care of an officer of the army, who, on account of ill health, was not on duty, and who took the child with him, as I have since understood, to his residence on or near the North river.

From the mouth of Seneca lake we proceeded, without the occurrence of any thing of importance, by the outlets of the Canandaigua, Honeoye, and Hemlock lakes, to the head of Connissius lake, where the army encamped on the ground that is now called Henderson's Flats.

Soon after the army had encamped, at the dusk of the evening, a party of twenty-one men, under the command of Lieut. Boyd, was detached from the rifle corps, and sent out for the purpose of reconnoitering the ground near the Genesee river, at a place now called Williamsburg, at a distance from the camp of about seven miles, under the guidance of a faithful Indian pilot. That place was then the site of an Indian village, and it was apprehended that the Indians and Rangers might be there or in that vicinity in considerable force.

On the arrival of the party at Williamsburg, they found that the Indian village had been recently deserted, as the fires in the huts were still burning. The night was so far spent when they got to their place of destination, that Lieutenant Boyd, considering the fatigue of his men, concluded to remain during the night near the village, and to send two men messengers with a report to the camp in the morning. Accordingly, a little before day-break, he despatched two men to the main body of the army, with information that the enemy had not been discovered.

After day-light, Lieut. Boyd cautiously crept from the place of his concealment, and upon getting a view of the village, discovered two Indians hovering about the settlement: one of whom was immediately shot and scalped by one of the riflemen, whose name was Murphy. Supposing that if there were Indians in that vicinity, or near the village, they would be instantly alarmed by this occurrence, Lieut. Boyd thought it most prudent to retire, and make the best of his way to the general encampment of our army. They accordingly set out and retraced the steps which they had taken the day before, till they were intercepted by the enemy.

On their arriving within about one mile and a half of the main army, they were surprized by the sudden appearance of a body of Indians, to the amount of five hundred, under the command of the celebrated Brandt, and the same number of Rangers, commanded by the infamous Butler, who had secreted themselves in a ravine of considerable extent, which lay across the track that Lieut. Boyd had pursued.

Upon discovering the enemy, and knowing that the only chance for escape was by breaking through their line, (one of the most desperate enterprizes ever undertaken,) Lieut. Boyd, after a few words of encouragement, led his men to the attempt. As extraordinary as it may seem, the first onset, though unsuccessful, was made without the loss of a man on the part of the heroic band, though several of the enemy were killed. Two attempts more were made, which were equally unsuccessful, and in which the whole party fell, except Lieut. Boyd, and eight others. Lieut. Boyd and a soldier by the name of Parker, were taken prisoners on the spot, a part of the remainder fled, and a part fell on the ground, apparently dead, and were overlooked by the Indians, who were too much engaged in pursuing the fugitives to notice those who fell.

When Lieut. Boyd found himself a prisoner, he solicited an interview with Brandt, whom he well knew commanded the Indians. This Chief, who was at that moment near, immediately presented himself, when Lieut. Boyd, by one of those appeals which are known only by those who have been initiated and instructed in certain mysteries, and which never fail to bring succor to a "distressed brother," addressed him as the only source from which he could expect a respite from cruel punishment or death. The appeal was recognized, and Brandt immediately, and in the strongest language, assured him that his life should be spared.

Lieut. Boyd, and his fellow-prisoner, Parker, were immediately conducted by a party of the Indians to the Indian village called Beard's Town, on the west side of Genesee river, in what is now called Leicester. After their arrival at Beard's Town, Brandt, their generous preserver, being called on service which required a few hours absence, left them in the care of the British Col. Butler, of the Rangers; who, as soon as Brandt had left them, commenced an interrogation, to obtain from the prisoners a statement of the number, situation and intentions of the army under Gen. Sullivan; and threatened them, in case they hesitated or prevaricated in their answers, to deliver them up immediately to be massacred by the Indians, who, in Brandt's absence, and with the encouragement of their more savage commander, Butler, were ready to commit the greatest cruelties. Relying, probably, on the promises which Brandt had made them, and which he undoubtedly meant to fulfil, they refused to give Butler the desired information. Butler, upon this, hastened to put his threat into execution. They were delivered to some of their most ferocious enemies, who, after having put them to very severe torture, killed them by severing their heads from their bodies.

The main army, immediately after hearing of the situation of Lieut. Boyd's detachment, moved on towards Genesee river, and finding the bodies of those who were slain in Boyd's heroic attempt to penetrate through the enemy's line, buried them in what is now the town of Groveland, where the grave is to be seen at this day.

Upon their arrival at the Genesee river, they crossed over, scoured the country for some distance on the river, burnt the Indian villages on the Genesee flats, and destroyed all their corn and other means of subsistence.

The bodies of Lieut. Boyd and Parker were found and buried near the bank of Beard's creek, under a bunch of wild plum-trees, on the road, as it now runs, from Moscow to Geneseo. I was one of those who committed to the earth the remains of my friend and companion in arms, the gallant Boyd.

Immediately after these events the army commenced its march back, by the same route that it came, to Tioga Point; thence down the Susquehanna to Wyoming; and thence across the country to Morristown, New-Jersey, where we went into winter quarters.

Gen. Sullivan's bravery is unimpeachable. He was unacquainted, however, with fighting the Indians, and made use of the best means to keep them at such a distance that they could not be brought into an engagement. It was his practice, morning and evening, to have cannon fired in or near the camp, by which the Indians were notified of their speed in marching, and of his situation, and were enabled to make a seasonable retreat.

The foregoing account, according to the best of my recollection is strictly correct.

JOHN SALMON.

Groveland, January 24, 1824.

Esq. Salmon was formerly from Northumberland county, Pennsylvania, and was first Serjeant in Capt. Simpson's and Lieut. Boyd's company.

✥◉✥◉✥

Tradition of the Origin of the Seneca Nation. Their Preservation from utter extinction. The Means by which the People who preceded the Senecas were destroyed—and the Cause of the different Indian Languages.

THE tradition of the Seneca Indians, in regard to their origin, as we are assured by Capt. Horatio Jones, who was a prisoner five years amongst them, and for many years since has been an interpreter, and agent for the payment of their annuities, is that they broke out of the earth from a large mountain at the head of Canandaigua Lake, and that mountain they still venerate as the place of their birth; thence they derive their name, "Ge-nun-de-wah,"* or Great Hill, and are called "The Great Hill People," which is the true definition of the word Seneca.

The great hill at the head of Canandaigua lake, from whence they sprung, is called Genundewah, and has for a long time past been the place where the Indians of that nation have met in council, to hold great talks, and to offer up prayers to the Great Spirit, on account of its having been their birth place; and also in consequence of the destruction of a serpent at that place, in ancient time, in a most miraculous manner, which threat-

*This by some is spoken Ge-nun-de-wah-gauh.

ened the destruction of the whole of the Senecas, and barely spared enough to commence replenishing the earth.

The Indians say, says Capt. Jones, that the fort on the big hill, or Genundewah, near the head of Canandaigua lake, was surrounded by a monstrous serpent, whose head and tail came together at the gate. A long time it lay there, confounding the people with its breath. At length they attempted to make their escape, some with their hommany-blocks, and others with different implements of household furniture; and in marching out of the fort walked down the throat of the serpent. Two orphan children, who had escaped this general destruction by being left some time before on the outside of the fort, were informed by an oracle of the means by which they could get rid of their formidable enemy—which was, to take a small bow and a poisoned arrow, made of a kind of willow, and with that shoot the serpent under its scales. This they did, and the arrow proved effectual; for on its penetrating the skin, the serpent became sick, and extending itself rolled down the hill, destroying all the timber that was in its way, disgorging itself and breaking wind greatly as it went. At every motion, a human head was discharged, and rolled down the hill into the lake, where they lie at this day, in a petrified state, having the hardness and appearance of stones.

To this day the Indians visit that sacred place, to mourn the loss of their friends, and to celebrate some rites that are peculiar to themselves. To the knowledge of white people there has been no timber on the great hill since it was first discovered by them, though it lay apparently in a state of nature for a great number of years, without cultivation. Stones in the shape of Indians' heads may be seen lying in the lake in great plenty, which are said to be the same that were deposited there at the death of the serpent.

The Senecas have a tradition, that previous to, and for some time after, their origin at Genundewah, this country, especially about the lakes, was thickly inhabited by a race of civil, enterprizing and industrious people, who were totally destroyed by the great serpent, that afterwards surrounded the great hill fort, with the assistance of others of the same species; and that they (the Senecas) went into possession of the improvements that were left.

In those days the Indians throughout the whole country, as the Senecas say, spoke one language; but having become considerably numerous, the before mentioned great serpent, by an unknown influence, confounded their language, so that they could not understand each other; which was the cause of their division into nations, as the Mohawks, Oneidas, &c. At that time, however, the Senecas retained their original language, and continued to occupy their mother hill, on which they fortified themselves against their enemies, and lived peaceably, till having offended the serpent,* they were cut off as before stated.

*The pagans of the Senecas believe that all the little snakes were made of the blood of the great serpent, after it rolled into the lake.

OF THEIR RELIGION—FEASTS—AND GREAT
SACRIFICE.

PERHAPS no people are more exact observers of religious duties than those Indians among the Senecas, who are denominated pagans, in contradistinction from those, who, having renounced some of their former superstitious notions, have obtained the name of Christians. The traditionary faith of their fathers, having been orally transmitted to them from time immemorial, is implicitly believed, scrupulously adhered to, and rigidly practised. They are agreed in their sentiments—are all of one order, and have individual and public good, especially among themselves, for the great motive which excites them to attend to those moral virtues that are directed and explained by all their rules, and in all their ceremonies.

Many years have elapsed since the introduction of Christian Missionaries among them, whom they have heard, and very generally understand the purport of the message they were sent to deliver. They say that it is highly probable that Jesus Christ came into the world in old times, to establish a religion that would promote the happiness of the white people, on the other side of the great water, (meaning the sea,) and that he died for the sins of his people, as the missionaries have informed them: But, they say that Jesus Christ had nothing to do with them, and that the Christian religion was not designed for their benefit; but rather, should they embrace it, they are confident it would make them worse, and consequently do them an injury. They say, also, that the Great Good Spirit gave them their religion; and that it is better adapted to their circumstances, situation and habits, and to the promotion of their present comfort and ultimate happiness, than any system that ever has or can be devised. They, however, believe, that the Christian religion is better calculated for the good of white people than theirs is; and wonder that those who have embraced it, do not attend more strictly to its precepts, and feel more engaged for its support and diffusion among themselves. At the present time, they are opposed to preachers or schoolmasters being sent or coming among them; and appear determined by all means to adhere to their ancient customs.

They believe in a Great Good Spirit, (whom they call in the Seneca language Nau-wan-e-u,) as the Creator of the world, and of every good thing —that he made men, and all inoffensive animals; that he supplies men with all the comforts of life; and that he is particularly partial to the Indians, whom they say are his peculiar people. They also believe that he is pleased in giving them (the Indians) good gifts; and that he is highly gratified with their good conduct—that he abhors their vices, and that he is willing to punish them for their bad conduct, not only in this world, but in a future state of existence. His residence, they suppose, lies at a great distance from them, in a country that is perfectly pleasant, where plenty abounds, even to profusion. That there the soil is completely fertile, and the seasons so mild that the corn never fails to be good—that the deer, elk, buffalo, turkies, and other useful animals, are numerous, and that the forests are well calculated to facilitate their hunting them with success—that the streams are pure, and abound with fish: and that nothing is wanting, to render fruition complete. Over this territory they say Nauwaneu presides as an all-powerful king; and that without counsel he admits to his pleasures all whom he considers to be worthy of enjoying so great a state of blessedness.

To this being they address prayers, offer sacrifices, give thanks for favors, and perform many acts of devotion and reverence.

They likewise believe that Nauwaneu has a brother that is less powerful than himself, and who is opposed to him, and to every one that is or wishes to be good: that this bad Spirit made all evil things, snakes, wolves, catamounts, and all other poisonous or noxious animals and beasts of prey, except the bear, which, on the account of the excellence of its meat for food, and skin for clothing, they say was made by Nauwaneu. Besides all this they say he makes and sends them their diseases, bad weather and bad crops, and that he makes and supports witches. He owns a large country adjoining that of his brother, with whom he is continually at variance. His fields are unproductive; thick clouds intercept the rays of the sun, and consequently destructive frosts are frequent; game is very scarce, and not easily taken; ravenous beasts are numerous; reptiles of every poisoned tooth lie in the path of the traveller; the streams are muddy, and hunger, nakedness and general misery, are severely felt by those who unfortunately become his tenants. He takes pleasure in afflicting the Indians here, and after their death receives all those into his dreary dominions, who in their life time have been so vile as to be rejected by Nauwaneu, under whose eye they are continued in an uncomfortable state forever. To this source of evil they offer some oblations to abate his vengeance, and render him propitious. They, however, believe him to be, in a degree, under subjection to his brother, and incapable of executing his plans only by his high permission.

Public religious duties are attended to in the celebration of particular festivals and sacrifices, which are observed with circumspection and attended with decorum.

In each year they have five feasts, or stated times for assembling in their tribes, and giving thanks to Nauwaneu, for the blessings which they have received from his kind and liberal and provident hand; and also to converse upon the best means of meriting a continuance of his favors. The first of these feasts is immediately after they have finished sugaring, at which time they give thanks for the favorable weather and great quantity of sap they have had, and for the sugar that they have been allowed to make for the benefit of their families. At this, as at all the succeeding feasts, the Chiefs arise singly, and address the audience in a kind of exhortation, in which they express their own thankfulness, urge the necessity and propriety of general gratitude, and point out the course which ought to be pursued by each individual, in order that Nauwaneu may continue to bless them, and that the evil spirit may be defeated.

On these occasions the Chiefs describe a perfectly straight line, half an inch wide, and perhaps ten miles long, which they direct their people to travel upon by placing one foot before the other, with the heel of one foot to the toe of the other, and so on till they arrive at the end. The meaning of which is, that they must not turn aside to the right hand or to the left into the paths of vice, but keep straight ahead in the way of well doing, that will lead them to the paradise of Nauwaneu.

The second feast is after planting; when they render thanks for the pleasantness of the season— for the good time they have had for preparing their ground and planting their corn; and are instructed by their Chiefs, by what means to merit a good harvest.

When the green corn becomes fit for use, they hold their third, or green corn feast. Their fourth is celebrated after corn harvest; and the fifth at the close of their year, and is always celebrated at the time of the old moon in the last of January or first of February. This last deserves a particular description.

The Indians having returned from hunting, and having brought in all the venison and skins that they have taken, a committee is appointed, says Mrs. Jemison, consisting of from ten to twenty active men, to superintend the festivities of the great sacrifice and thanksgiving that is to be immediately celebrated. This being done, preparations are made at the council-house, or place of meeting, for the reception and accommodation of the whole tribe; and then the ceremonies are commenced, and the whole is conducted with a great degree of order and harmony, under the direction of the committee.

Two white dogs,* without spot or blemish, are selected (if such can be found, and if not, two that have the fewest spots) from those belonging to the tribe, and killed near the door of the council-house, by being strangled. A wound on the animal or an effusion of blood, would spoil the victim, and render the sacrifice useless. The dogs are then painted red on their faces, edges of their ears, and on various parts of their bodies, and are curiously decorated with ribbons of different colors, and fine feathers, which are tied and fastened on in such a manner as to make the most elegant appearance. They are then hung on a post near the door of the council-house, at the height of twenty feet from the ground.

This being done, the frolic is commenced by those who are present, while the committee run through the tribe or town, and hurry the people to assemble, by knocking on their houses. At this time the committee are naked, (wearing only a breech-clout,) and each carries a paddle, with which he takes up ashes and scatters them about the house in every direction. In the course of the ceremonies, all the fire is extinguished in every hut throughout the tribe, and new fire, struck from the flint on

*This was the practice in former times; but at present I am informed that only one dog is sacrificed.

each hearth, is kindled, after having removed the whole of the ashes, old coals, &c. Having done this, and discharged one or two guns, they go on, and in this manner they proceed till they have visited every house in the tribe. This finishes the business of the first day.

On the second day the committee dance, go through the town with bear-skin on their legs, and at every time they start they fire a gun. They also beg through the tribe, each carrying a basket in which to receive whatever may be bestowed. The alms consist of Indian tobacco, and other articles that are used for incense at the sacrifice. Each manager at this time carries a dried tortoise or turtle shell, containing a few beans, which he frequently rubs on the walls of the houses, both inside and out. This kind of manœuvering by the committee continues two or three days, during which time the people at the council-house recreate themselves by dancing.

On the fourth or fifth day the committee make false faces of husks, in which they run about, making a frightful but ludicrous appearance. In this dress, (still wearing the bear-skin,) they run to the council-house, smearing themselves with dirt and bedaub every one who refuses to contribute something towards filling the baskets of incense, which they continue to carry, soliciting alms. During all this time they collect the evil spirit, or drive it off entirely, for the present, and also concentrate within themselves all the sins of their tribe, however numerous or heinous.

On the eighth or ninth day, the committee having received all the sin, as before observed, into their own bodies, they take down the dogs, and after having transfused the whole of it into one of their own number, he, by a peculiar slight of hand, or kind of magic, works it all out of himself into the dogs. The dogs, thus loaded with all the sins of the people, are placed upon a pile of wood that is directly set on fire. Here they are burnt, together with the sins with which they were loaded, surrounded by the multitude, who throw incense of tobacco or the like into the fire, the scent of which they say, goes up to Nauwaneu, to whom it is pleasant and acceptable.

This feast continues nine days,* and during that time the Chiefs review the national affairs of the year past; agree upon the best plan to be pursued through the next year, and attend to all internal regulations.

On the last day, the whole company partake of an elegant dinner, consisting of meat, corn and beans, boiled together in large kettles, and stirred till the whole is completely mixed and soft. This mess is devoured without much ceremony—some eat with a spoon, by dipping out of the kettles; others serve themselves in small dippers; some in one way, and some in another, till the whole is consumed. After this they perform the war dance, the peace dance, and smoke the pipe of peace; and then, free from iniquity, each repairs to his place

---

*At present, as I have been informed, this feast is not commonly held more than from five to seven days. In former times, and till within a few years, nine days were particularly observed.

of abode, prepared to commence the business of a new year. In this feast, temperance is observed, and commonly, order prevails in a greater degree than would naturally be expected.

They are fond of the company of spectators who are disposed to be decent, and treat them politely in their way; but having been frequently imposed upon by the whites, they treat them generally with indifference.

❖◯❖◯❖

OF THEIR DANCES.

OF these, two only will be noticed. The war dance is said to have originated about the time that the Six Nations, or Northern Indians, commenced the old war with the Cherokees and other Southern Indian Nations, about one hundred years ago.

When a tribe, or number of tribes of the Six Nations, had assembled for the purpose of going to battle with their enemies, the Chiefs sung this song, and accompanied the music with dancing, and gestures that corresponded with the sentiments expressed, as a kind of stimulant to increase their courage, and anxiety to march forward to the place of carnage.

Those days having passed away, the Indians at this day sing the 'war song,' to commemorate the achievements of their fathers, and as a kind of amusement. When they perform it, they arm themselves with a war-club, tomahawk and knife, and commence singing with firm voice, and a stern, resolute countenance: but before they get through they exhibit in their features and actions the most shocking appearance of anger, fury and vengeance, that can be imagined: No exhibition of the kind can be more terrifying to a stranger.

The song requires a number of repetitions in the tune, and has a chorus that is sung at the end of each verse. I have not presumed to arrange it in metre; but the following is the substance: "We are assembled in the habiliments of war, and will go in quest of our enemies. We will march to their land and spoil their possessions. We will take their women and children, and lead them into captivity. The warriors shall fall by our war-clubs—we will give them no quarter. Our tomahawks we will dip in their brains! with our scalping knives we will scalp them." At each period comes on the chorus, which consists of one monosyllable only, that is sounded a number of times, and articulated like a faint, stifled groan. This word is "eh," and signifies "we will," or "we will go," or "we will do." While singing, they perform the ceremony of killing and scalping, with a great degree of dexterity.

The peace dance is performed to a tune without words, by both sexes. The Indians stand erect in one place, and strike the floor with the heel and toes of one foot, and then of the other, (the heels and toes all the while nearly level,) without changing their position in the least. The squaws at the same time perform it by keeping the feet close together, and without raising them from the ground, move a short distance to the right, and then to the left, by first moving their toes and then their heels. This dance is beautiful, and is generally attended with decency.

APPENDIX

OF THEIR GOVERNMENT.

THEIR government is an oligarchy of a mixed nature; and is administered by Chiefs, a part of whose offices are hereditary, and a part elective. The nation is divided into tribes, and each tribe commonly has two Chiefs. One of these inherits his office from his father. He superintends all civil affairs in the tribe; attends the national council, of which he is a member; assents to all conveyances of land, and is consulted on every subject of importance. The other is elected by the tribe, and can be removed at the pleasure of his constituents for malconduct. He also is a member of the national council: but his principal business is to superintend the military concerns of his tribe, and in war to lead his warriors to battle. He acts in concert with the other Chief, and their word is implicitly relied on, as the law by which they must be governed. That which they prohibit, is not meddled with. The Indian laws are few, and easily expounded. Their business of a public nature is transacted in council, where every decision is final. They meet in general council once a year, and sometimes oftener. The administration of their government is not attended with expense. They have no national revenue, and consequently have no taxes. ❖❍❖❍❖

THE EXTENT AND NUMBER OF THE SIX NATIONS.

THE Six Nations in the state of New-York are located upon several reservations, from the Oneida Lake to the Cattaraugus and Allegany rivers.

A part of those nations live on the Sandusky, in the state of Ohio, viz—380 Cayugas, 100 Senecas, 64 Mohawks, 64 Oneidas, and 80 Onondagas. The bulk of the Mohawks are on Grand River, Upper Canada, together with some Senecas, Tuscaroras, Cayugas, Oneidas, and Onondagas.

In the state of New-York there are 5000, and in the state of Ohio 688, as we are assured by Capt. Horatio Jones, agent for paying their annuities, making in the whole, in both states, 5688.

❖◯❖◯❖

OF THEIR COURTSHIPS, &c.

WHEN an Indian sees a squaw whom he fancies, he sends a present to her mother or parents, who on receiving it consult with his parents, his friends, and each other, on the propriety and expediency of the proposed connexion. If it is not agreeable, the present is returned; but if it is, the lover is informed of his good fortune, and immediately goes to live with her, or takes her to a hut of his own preparing.

Polygamy is practised in a few instances, and is not prohibited.

Divorces are frequent. If a difficulty of importance arises between a married couple, they agree to separate. They divide their property and children; the squaw takes the girls, the Indian the boys, and both are at liberty to marry again.

They have no marriage ceremony, nor form of divorcement, other than what has been mentioned.

A P P E N D I X

OF FAMILY GOVERNMENT.

In their families, parents are very mild, and the mother superintends the children. The word of the Indian father, however, is law, and must be obeyed by the whole that are under his authority. One thing respecting the Indian women is worthy of attention, and perhaps of imitation, although it is now a days considered beneath the dignity of the ladies, especially those who are the most refined; and that is, they are under a becoming subjection to their husbands. It is a rule, inculcated in all the Indian tribes, and practised throughout their generations, that a squaw shall not walk before her Indian, nor pretend to take the lead in his business. And for this reason we never can see a party on the march to or from hunting and the like, in which the squaws are not directly in the rear of their partners.

❖◯❖◯❖

OF THEIR FUNERALS.

The deceased having been laid out in his best clothing, is put into a coffin of boards or bark, and with him is deposited, in every instance, a small cup and a cake. Generally two or three candles are also put into the coffin, and in a few instances, at the burial of a great man, all his implements of war are buried by the side of the body. The coffin is then closed and carried to the grave. On its being let down, the person who takes the lead of the solemn transaction, or a Chief, addresses the dead in a short speech, in which he charges him not to be troubled about himself in his new situation, nor on his journey, and not to trouble his friends, wife or children, whom he has left. Tells him that if he meets with strangers on his way, he must inform them what tribe he belongs to, who his relatives are, the situation in which he left them, and that having done this, he must keep on till he arrives at the good fields in the country of Nauwaneu. That when he arrives there he will see all his ancestors and personal friends that have gone before him; who, together with all the Chiefs of celebrity, will receive him joyfully, and furnish him with every article of perpetual happiness.

The grave is now filled and left till evening, when some of the nearest relatives of the dead build a fire at the head of it, near which they set till morning. In this way they continue to practise nine successive nights, when, believing that their departed friend has arrived at the end of his journey, they discontinue their attention. During this time the relatives of the dead are not allowed to dance.

Formerly, frolics were held, after the expiration of nine days, for the dead, at which all the squaws got drunk, and those were the only occasions on which they were intoxicated: but lately those are discontinued, and squaws feel no delicacy in getting inebriated.

❖◯❖◯❖

OF THEIR CREDULITY.

As ignorance is the parent of credulity, it is not a thing to be wondered at that the Indians should possess it in a great degree, and even suffer themselves to be dictated and governed by it in many of the most important transactions of their lives.

They place great confidence in dreams, attach some sign to every uncommon circumstance, and believe in charms, spirits, and many supernatural things that never existed, only in minds enslaved to ignorance and tradition: but in no instance is their credulity so conspicuous, as in their unalterable belief in witches.

They believe there are many of these, and that next to the author of evil, they are the greatest scourge to their people. The term witch, by them, is used both in the masculine and feminine gender, and denotes a person to whom the evil deity has delegated power to inflict diseases, cause death, blast corn, bring bad weather, and in short to cause almost any calamity to which they are liable. With this impression, and believing that it is their actual duty to destroy, as far as lies in their power, every source of unhappiness, it has been a custom among them from time immemorial, to destroy every one that they could convict of so heinous a crime; and in fact there is no reprieve from the sentence.

Mrs. Jemison informed us that more or less who had been charged with being witches, had been executed in almost every year since she has lived on the Genesee. Many, on being suspected, made their escape: while others, before they were aware of being implicated, have been apprehended and brought to trial. She says that a number of years ago, an Indian chased a squaw, near Beard's Town, and caught her; but on the account of her great strength she got away. The Indian, vexed and disappointed, went home, and the next day reported that he saw her have fire in her mouth, and that she was a witch. Upon this she was apprehended and killed immediately. She was Big-tree's cousin. Mrs. Jemison says she was present at the execution. She also saw one other killed and thrown into the river.

Col. Jeremiah Smith, of Leicester, near Beard's Town, saw an Indian killed by his five brothers, who struck him on the head with their tomahawks at one time. He was charged with being a witch, because of his having been fortunate enough, when on a hunting party, to kill a number of deer, while his comrades failed of taking any.

Col. Smith also saw a squaw, who had been convicted of being a witch, killed by having small green whips burnt till they were red hot, but not quite coaled, and thrust down her throat. From such trifling causes thousands have lost their lives, and notwithstanding the means that are used for their reformation, the pagans will not suffer "a witch to live."

❖◯❖◯❖

OF THE MANNER OF FARMING, AS PRACTISED BY THE INDIAN WOMEN.

It is well known that the squaws have all the labor of the field to perform, and almost every other kind of hard service, which, in civil society, is performed by the men. In order to expedite their business, and at the same time enjoy each other's company, they all work together in one field, or at whatever job they may have on hand. In the spring they choose an old active squaw to be their driver and overseer when at labor, for the ensuing year. She accepts the honor, and they consider themselves bound to obey her.

When the time for planting arrives, and the soil is prepared, the squaws are assembled in the morning, and conducted into a field, where each plants one row. They then go into the next field, and plant once across, and so on till they have gone through the tribe. If any remains to be planted, they again commence where they did at first, (in the same field,) and so keep on till the whole is finished. By this rule they perform their labor of every kind, and every jealousy of one having done more or less than another, is effectually avoided.

Each squaw cuts her own wood; but it is all brought to the house under the direction of the overseer—each bringing one back load.

❖◉❖◉❖

OF THEIR METHOD OF COMPUTING TIME, AND
KEEPING THEIR RECORDS.

THIS is done by moons and winters: a moon is a month, and the time from the end of one winter to that of another, a year.

From sunset till sunrise, they say that the sun is asleep. In the old of the moon, when it does not shine in the night, they say it is dead. They rejoice greatly at the sight of the new moon.

In order to commemorate great events, and preserve the chronology of them, the war Chief in each tribe keeps a war post. This post is a peeled stick of timber, 10 or 12 feet high, that is erected in the town. For a campaign they make, or rather the Chief makes, a perpendicular red mark, about three inches long and half an inch wide; on the opposite side from this, for a scalp, they make a red cross, thus, +; on another side, for a prisoner taken alive, they make a red cross in this manner, $\overset{\cdot}{\times}$, with a head or dot, and by placing such significant hireoglyphics in so conspicuous a situation, they are enabled to ascertain with great certainty the time and circumstances of past events.

Hiokatoo had a war-post, on which was recorded his military exploits, and other things that he tho't worth preserving.

❖◯❖◯❖

ANECDOTES.

HIOKATOO used to say that when he was a young man, there lived in the same tribe with him an old Indian warrior, who was a great counsellor, by the name of Buck-in-je-hil-lish. Buckinjehillish having, with great fatigue, attended the council when it was deliberating upon war, declared that none but the ignorant made war, but that the wise men and the warriors had to do the fighting. This speech exasperated his countrymen to such a degree that he was apprehended and tried for being a witch, on the account of his having lived to so advanced an age; and because he could not show some reason why he had not died before, he was sentenced to be tomahawked by a boy on the spot, which was accordingly done.

IN the last war, (1814,) an Indian who had been on fatigue, called at a commissary's and begged some bread. He was sent for a pail of water before he received it, and while he was absent an officer told the commissary to put a piece of money into the bread, and observe the event. He did so. The Indian took the bread and went off: but on the next day having ate his bread and found the money, he came to the commissary and gave him the same, as the officer had anticipated.

LITTLE BEARD, a celebrated Indian Chief, having arrived to a very advanced age, died at his town on the Genesee river about the first of June, 1806, and was buried after the manner of burying chiefs. In his life time he had been quite arbitrary, and had made some enemies whom he hated, probably, and was not loved by them. The grave, however, deprives envy of its malignity, and revenge of its keenness.

Little Beard had been dead but a few days when the great eclipse of the sun took place, on the sixteenth of June, which excited in the Indians a great degree of astonishment; for as they were ignorant of astronomy, they were totally unqualified to account for so extraordinary a phenomenon. The crisis was alarming, and something effectual must be done, without delay, to remove, if possible, the cause of such coldness and darkness, which it was expected would increase. They accordingly ran together in the three towns near the Genesee river, and after a short consultation agreed that Little Beard, on the account of some old grudge which he yet cherished towards them, had placed himself between them and the sun, in order that their corn might not grow, and so reduce them to a state of starvation. Having thus found the cause, the next thing was to remove it, which could only be done by the use of powder and ball. Upon this, every gun and rifle was loaded, and a firing commenced, that continued without cessation till the old fellow left his seat, and the obscurity was entirely removed, to the great joy of the ingenious and fortunate Indians.

In the month of February, 1824, Corn Planter, a learned pagan Chief at Tonnewonta, died of common sickness. He had received a liberal education, and was held in high estimation in his town and tribe, by both parties; but the pagans more particularly mourned his loss deeply, and seemed entirely unreconciled. They imputed his death to witchcraft, and charged an Indian by the name of Prompit, with the crime.

Mr. Prompit is a christian Indian, of the Tuscarora nation, who has lived at Tonnewonta a number of years, where he has built a saw-mill himself, which he owns, and is considered a decent, respectable man.

About two weeks after the death of Corn Planter, Mr. Prompit happened in company where the author was present, and immediately begun to converse upon that subject. He said that the old fashioned Indians called him a witch—believed that he had killed Corn Planter, and had said that they would kill him. But, said he, all good people know that I am not a witch, and that I am clear of the charge. Likely enough they will kill me; but if they do, my hands are clean, my conscience is clear, and I shall go up to God. I will not run nor hide from them, and they may kill me if they choose to—I am innocent. When Jesus Christ's enemies, said he, wanted to kill him, he did not run away from them, but let them kill him; and why should I run away from my enemies?

How the affair will terminate, we are unable to decide.

❖◐❖◑❖

DESCRIPTION OF GENESEE RIVER AND ITS BANKS, FROM MOUNT MORRIS TO THE UPPER FALLS.

From Mount Morris the banks of the Genesee are from two to four hundred feet in height, with narrow flats on one side of the river or the other, till you arrive at the tract called Gardow, or Cross Hills. Here you come to Mrs. Jemison's flats, which are two miles and a quarter long, and from eighty to one hundred and twenty rods wide, lying mostly on the west side of the river.

Near the upper end of these flats is the Great Slide. Directly above this, the banks (still retaining their before mentioned height) approach so near each other as to admit of but thirty acres of flat on one side of the river only, and above this the perpendicular rock comes down to the water.

From Gardow you ascend the river five miles to the lower falls, which are ninety-three feet perpendicular. These falls are twenty rods wide, and have the greatest channel on the east side. From

Wolf creek to these falls the banks are covered with elegant white and Norway pine.

Above the lower falls the banks for about two miles are of perpendicular rock, and retain their height of between two and four hundred feet. Having travelled this distance you reach the middle falls, which are an uninterrupted sheet of water fifteen rods wide, and one hundred and ten feet in perpendicular height. This natural curiosity is not exceeded by any thing of the kind in the western country, except the cataract at Niagara.

From the middle falls the banks gradually rise, till you ascend the river half a mile, when you come to the upper falls, which are somewhat rolling, 66 feet, in the shape of a harrow. Above this the banks are of moderate height. The timber from the lower to the upper falls is principally pine. Just above the middle falls a saw-mill was erected this season (1823) by Messrs. Ziba Hurd and Alva Palmer. ❖◉❖◉❖

HUNTING ANECDOTE.

In November, 1822, Capt. Stephen Rolph and Mr. Alva Palmer drove a deer into Genesee river, a short distance above the middle falls, where the banks were so steep and the current so impetuous, that it could not regain the shore, and consequently was precipitated over the falls, one hundred and ten feet, into the gulph below. The hunters ran along the bank below the falls, to watch the fate of the animal, expecting it would be dashed in pieces. But to their great astonishment it came up alive, and by swimming across a small eddy, reached the bank almost under the falls; and as it stood in that situation, Capt. Rolph, who was on the top of the bank, shot it. This being done, the next thing to be considered was, how to get their prize. The rock being perpendicular, upwards of one hundred feet, would not admit of their climbing down to it, and there was no way, apparently, for them to get at it, short of going down the river two miles, to the lower falls, and then by creeping between the water and the precipice, they might possibly reach their game. This process would be too tedious. At length Mr. Palmer proposed to Capt. Rolph and Mr. Heman Merwin, who had joined them, that if they would make a windlas and fasten it to a couple of saplings that stood near, and then procure some ropes, he would be let down and get the deer. The apparatus was prepared; the rope was tied round Palmer's body, and he was let down. On arriving at the bottom he unloosed himself, fastened the rope round the deer, which they drew up, and then threw down the rope, in which he fastened himself, and was drawn up, without having sustained any injury. From the top to the bottom of the rock, where he was let down, was exactly one hundred and twenty feet.

FINIS.